MEN OF HONOR AND INFLUENCE

Other Shaw Books by Stuart Briscoe:

The Apostles' Creed

Discipleship for Ordinary People

The Fruit of the Spirit

The Fruit of the Spirit (Fisherman Bible Studyguide)

Genuine People

Nine Attitudes That Keep a Christian Going and Growing

1 Peter: Living in a Hostile World

Philippians: Happiness beyond Our Happenings

Secrets of Spiritual Stamina

The Sermon on the Mount

The Ten Commandments

The Ten Commandments (Fisherman Bible Studyguide)

Titus: Living as God's Very Own People

Transforming the Daily Grind

STUART BRISCOE

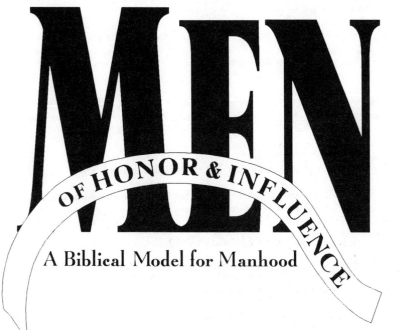

MEN
OF HONOR & INFLUENCE

A Biblical Model for Manhood

Harold Shaw Publishers
Wheaton, Illinois

All Scripture quotations, unless otherwise indicated, are taken from the *Holy Bible, New International Version*™. NIV™. Copyright © 1973, 1978, 1984 by the International Bible Society. Used by permission of Zondervan Publishing House. All rights reserved.

Scripture quotations marked TEV are from *Today's English Version (The Good News Bible)*, © 1966, 1971, 1976, 1992 American Bible Society. Used by permission.

Because Stuart Briscoe's materials are widely published, it is difficult to avoid some duplication of content. While all the material here has been reworked for this volume, some chapters have appeared in two other Shaw books: *Genuine People: Living and Relating as Real Christians* (1995) or *The Sermon on the Mount* (1995).

A version of chapter 6, "Men Working," appeared in *Choices for a Lifetime: Determining the Values That Will Shape Your Future* © 1995 by Stuart Briscoe. Used by permission of Tyndale House Publishers, Inc., Wheaton, IL 60189.

ISBN 0-87788-549-4

Edited by Verne Becker and Robert Bittner

Cover design by David LaPlaca

Library of Congress Cataloging-in-Publication Data

Briscoe, D. Stuart.
   Men of honor and influence : a Biblical model for manhood / by Stuart Briscoe.
     p. cm.
   ISBN 0-87788-549-4
   1. Men—Religious life. I. Title.
   BV4528.2.B76 1996
   248.8'42—dc20   96-21042
                                             CIP

03 02 01 00 99 98 97 96

10 9 8 7 6 5 4 3 2 1

Contents

1   A Man after God's Own Heart 7

2   The Meaning of Manhood 19

Values of a Christian Man

3   Faithfulness: Following the Will of God....33

4   Focus: Making God Our First Priority 43

5   Fortitude: Standing Up to Temptation........51

The Roles of a Christian Man

6   Men Working 65

7   The Provider's Duty...................................79

8   What Do Real Husbands Do? 95

9   Fathers and Their Children.......................105

10   The Cost of Friendship............................123

11   Men Worth Their Salt..............................141

The Lord has sought out a man after his own
heart and appointed him leader of his people.

1 Samuel 13:14

The Lord does not look at the things man looks
at. Man looks at the outward appearance, but the
Lord looks at the heart.

1 Samuel 16:7

❖❖❖

1

A Man after God's Own Heart

Perhaps the highest praise a man could ever receive is to be called "a man after God's own heart." The Lord himself used these words to describe his servant David, the man who would succeed Saul as king of Israel. They can also serve as a goal men can strive for today.

But what does it really mean in today's world to be a man after God's own heart? To answer this question, let us compare the lives of the two men mentioned in the passages quoted above—Saul, who ultimately did not follow after God's heart, and David, who did.

The Meaning of *Heart*

We use the word *heart* in many ways today. Somebody is good at heart. We learn things by heart. If we are courageous, we have a heart of oak. If we are afraid, our heart is in our mouth. If we want someone to show a little compassion, we say, "Come on, have a heart." If we are deeply attached to someone or something, we might say, "I gave you my heart." If we have a tremendous desire for something, we set our heart on acquiring it. If we take something seriously, we take it to heart. Someone who is very open and transparent wears his heart on his sleeve. And if people are deeply involved in something, they get into it with all their heart.

Our contemporary use of the word *heart* is closely aligned to the biblical use. The heart is the innermost part of our being that God has specifically and uniquely designed to do all things in accordance with his will. It is the measure of our integrity, of who we are as a human being.

In the early chapters of 1 Samuel, where we learn about God's dealings with Samuel, Saul, and David, we can see how often the heart plays a role in what God has to say. There is a wonderful sentence in 1 Samuel 12:20, when Samuel tells the Israelites, "Do not be afraid. . . . You have done all this evil; yet do not turn away from the Lord, but serve the Lord with all your heart." Yes, you have done evil, this passage admits, but that does not mean that your heart cannot once again turn fully back to God. No matter what the heart has desired in the past, it can once again desire God and God's will.

Throughout Scripture the heart helps people discern the truth about God. It is open to discover all that God has revealed of himself. To serve the Lord with all our heart means that we desire to serve him. Then, we must decide to turn toward his way and away from all that is contrary to it. Finally, we must dedicate ourselves to follow through on that which we have decided.

We probably know enough about our heart—our innermost being—to realize that often we are not prepared to discern the truth about God. We won't take the time. Or perhaps we discern the truth but do not desire to do it. We desire our own way instead. Often we have a desire, but we are not willing to make the sometimes difficult decisions that need to be made. We back away from them. And sometimes we make decisions, but do not dedicate ourselves to following through with them. Therefore the heart, created by God to carry out all that he has in mind for us, can wind up leading us in the opposite direction.

What does it mean to be a man after God's own heart? We are never given an exact description of what God means by this, but we know that David was such a man. We also know that Saul was not. In God's evaluation, something was wrong with Saul's heart.

Saul's Heart

The first symptom of Saul's "heart problem" was that he lacked dependence upon God. The facts are found in 1 Samuel 13:1-15. I imagine the conversation described in these verses between Saul and the prophet Samuel going something like this:

"Now listen, Saul," Samuel says, "you go away to Gilgal for seven days and wait for me there. Don't do anything till I come, and when I come I will tell you exactly what the Lord wants you to do. Have you got that?"

"Got it," says Saul.

"What do you have to do again?"

"I've got to wait seven days and I mustn't do anything until you come and tell me what God wants me to do."

Seven days go by, and it is getting close to the end of the seventh day. No Samuel. Saul is getting nervous and anxious. His troops are deserting him. So rather than wait for the prophet to show up, he takes matters into his own hands and offers up the sacrifice himself.

It may seem like a small matter to us, but as God examines Saul's heart, he sees more than an isolated act of independence—he sees a fundamental heart attitude. When it comes down to the crunch, Saul is going to do what he wants to do. He is impetuous and confident of his own wisdom. He has a heart for doing his own thing.

Saul's second problem surfaces in 1 Samuel 15. This is a horrible, difficult story. For reasons we cannot understand, God told Saul to destroy the Amalekites, wiping out everyone, even the livestock. Yet Saul chose partial obedience. He obeyed God's command to a point, then disobeyed when it came to those things he did not want to do. Not only was Saul suspect in the area of dependence, he was decidedly suspect in the area of obedience.

As Christians, there are really only two things we absolutely have to do: We must depend on God's strength and obey his word. If we struggle with dependence and don't like being obedient, we have major heart problems. Unless those problems are fixed, we will never become the kind of men God wants us to be, living the lives God wants us to live.

Yet Saul's difficulties do not end there. He also is suspect in the exercise of his conscience. For instance, in 1 Samuel 15:13-14 he is ready to mislead God's prophet Samuel, conveying false impressions about the raid on the Amalekites. After that raid—where he did only what he wanted to do, not what God told him to do—he went to Samuel and said, "Hallelujah! Praise the Lord! We've had a great time and we've done what the Lord told us to do!"

Samuel looked at him and said, "If you have done all that God told you to do, why do I still hear oxen lowing? Why do I hear sheep bleating? If you had followed God's instructions, there would be no oxen and no sheep here."

Saul knew he was being disobedient. His conscience was no doubt telling him, "Saul, don't pretend. God knows your heart. Samuel's got a discerning spirit; he will see right through you." But Saul pretended anyway.

Saul plugged on, apparently having no qualms about communicating false information. When Samuel questioned him about why he had not followed God's instructions to destroy everything, Saul answered, "It wasn't me who did it—it was the soldiers. They decided to keep some of the best stuff so that we might offer it to the Lord." Neither of these things was true. The soldiers did not make the decision, nor did they set aside the plunder for God; they had reserved it for themselves.

As if this were not bad enough, Saul is able to look Samuel in the eye and claim a false integrity. Even after he had been exposed, he stuck to his story. Denying the truth, he put on pious attitudes and said, "But I did obey the Lord" (1 Sam. 15:20).

Samuel shook his head. "I'm sorry, Saul, you are through. You are not exhibiting the kind of heart that God is looking for. You aren't concerned with the things of God. You have no attitude of dependence or obedience. You don't even want a clear conscience. You're not a man after God's own heart."

That is a powerful message. But dependence, obedience, and integrity are the things God requires in a man who is after God's own heart. Despite his own shortcomings and sins, David was such a man.

David's Heart

In contrast to Saul, David provides us with a positive

example of a man after God's own heart. David was not perfect. But from God's perspective, his heart was in the right place even though his behavior was sometimes in the wrong place.

We can learn a lot about David's heart by reading the Psalms that he wrote. For example, in Psalm 61:1-4, we can see the difference between Saul's heart and David's heart. Whereas Saul chose to act independently of God, David was able to write:

Hear my cry, O God;
listen to my prayer.
From the ends of the earth I call to you,
I call as my heart grows faint;
lead me to the rock that is higher than I.
For you have been my refuge,
a strong tower against the foe.
I long to dwell in your tent forever
and take refuge in the shelter of your wings.

What a contrast to the man who said to himself, "I don't need to wait on God. I'll do it my way and then ask God's blessing on it." A man after God's own heart knows how weak and sinful and weary his heart can be. He knows himself. He suspects himself. But in that knowing and suspecting he becomes utterly dependent on the Lord, and he calls upon him.

In addition, David is developing an obedient heart. In Psalm 40:8 he writes, "I desire to do your will, O my God; your law is within my heart." He desires above all else that he might learn what it means to be obedient. He desires to find more and more ways in which he can honestly discover God's will and do it. Of course, David is as weak and sinful as Saul and the rest of us. Still, he is seeking after an honest heart.

I love to visit Anglican churches and experience their beautiful liturgy. Just before the priest begins his homily, he offers up the words of David as a prayer: "May the words of my mouth and the meditation of my heart be pleasing in your sight, O Lord, my Rock and my Redeemer" (Ps. 19:14). This is the language of an honest heart. Deep down, David wants to be in tune with what the Lord has in mind for him—in the words of his mouth, in the meditations of his heart, in the inner mechanics of his life.

Finally, David demonstrates an open and honest heart of integrity before God. In Psalm 139 he closes by saying, "Search me, O God, and know my heart; test me and know my anxious thoughts. See if there is any offensive way in me, and lead me in the way everlasting" (vv. 23-24).

Do you know what God is looking for in our world today? More and more men with a heart like David, a heart after God's own heart.

Inside Out

A bit further on in 1 Samuel, God makes another statement about the heart that speaks to the situation of men today. He has just sent Samuel to Jesse and told him that he has chosen one of Jesse's sons to be the next king. One by one the older sons parade before Samuel, who thinks that surely one of these able-bodied men must be God's choice. But God says to him, "The Lord does not look at the things man looks at. Man looks at the outward appearance, but the Lord looks at the heart" (1 Sam. 16:7).

One of the hardest lessons we have to learn is that God is infinitely more concerned about the internals than the externals. Many of us have become wrapped up in image making, in packaging, in projecting what we want to project and marketing what we want to market. More than any previous generation, we may be the one that is primarily concerned with external appearance at the expense of what really goes on in the heart.

God is far more concerned about character than he is about reputation. Reputation is what people think we are. Character is what God knows we are. He is interested in the reality behind all our packaging and promoting and projecting. The difference between character and reputation should burn in our hearts and minds.

Two Dangers of the Heart

As men seeking to lead godly lives of honor and influence, we should constantly be guarding ourselves against two dangers—a hardened heart and a hypocritical heart.

Remember the story of God's dealings with Pharaoh? Pharaoh was a classic case of a man with a hardened heart. Again and again he agreed to let God's people go free from their slavery in Egypt, and then he reneged on it. He hardened his heart. So God brought judgment on him, and Pharaoh repented. But when the judgment stopped, when the pressure was off, he hardened his heart again.

We might get the impression from this story that Pharaoh always had the opportunity to soften his hard heart and turn back to God. I do not think that is necessarily true. God will give people an awful lot of rope to harden their heart, but when it has gone too far he could say, "All right, you have had all the opportunities to change that you are going to get." After Pharaoh had hardened his heart again and again and again, God said, "If that is what you want, then that is what you'll have." And God hardened his heart permanently.

Contrast the hardened heart of Pharaoh with that of the king mentioned in Proverbs—probably David's son Solomon—who wrote, "The king's heart is in the hand of the Lord; he directs it like a watercourse wherever he pleases" (Prov. 21:1). Like King David, this king had given his heart to the Lord—open, willing, ready, eager—and the Lord had taken it and was directing it in the path of his choice.

Not only must we guard against a hardened heart, we must also watch for a hypocritical heart. During his lifetime, Jesus encountered more hypocritical hearts among the Pharisees than any other group. They meticulously observed the law, but were so wrapped up in external matters of religion—eating only certain foods, walking certain distances, finding ways to cut corners while giving the impression of being absolutely correct—that they overlooked internal matters of much greater importance. Jesus summarized their hypocrisy in an unforgettable expression. He said, "You strain out a gnat but swallow a camel" (Matt. 23:24). In other words, when it came to religious nitpicking, the Pharisees were the biggest nitters and pickers in the world. But while they were nitting and picking, their hearts were far from the Lord. That's a terrible danger for anyone.

God is not looking for a perfect heart, because he knows he will not find one. Rather, he is looking for the heart of an honest, genuine, heartbroken person who can say,

"Lord, when I consider myself before you—and I know my heart before you, and I see how wrongly I discern and how unwisely I desire and how badly I decide and how inadequately I'm dedicated—my heart breaks before you. I humble myself and ask that my heart might be placed in your mighty hand, so that you might touch it and change it."

It is easy for us to go through the motions and yet hold onto a hard heart. It is easy to meet people's expectations and still have a hypocritical heart. But we are on dangerous ground when the heart is wrong in the realm of religion.

The Heart and Relationships

We men must also pay attention to our heart in the realm of relationships. Consider these questions: What do I want for my family? What do I want for my children and grandchildren? A good education? A fulfilling job? A nice home? Is this what I want most for them? Or do I have an overwhelming desire for my kids to become men and women after God's own heart?

If that is what you want for your kids, make sure your family knows where your priorities lie. If you focus on externals, they may get the impression that how they appear is more important than who they are. They may think that all you are concerned about is that they look right and behave right, and that you don't really care what they are like on the inside.

For those thinking of marriage: What do you want in a spouse? Well, you think, she's got to be cute, smart, and it would be nice if she had money. There's nothing wrong with any of these things, but if they become your main criteria, God help you. You may find someone who is beautiful and smart and rich—and who has no heart for God whatsoever.

What do you look for in an employee?

What do you want in a friend? And what do you know of yourself?

As we strive to be men after God's own heart, may we always keep in mind the stark contrast between the heart of Saul and the heart of David. And may we always allow Jesus Christ—truly a man after God's own heart—to dwell in our hearts through faith, empowering us to be *godly* men. In the next chapter we will explore the second half of that phrase "godly men," taking a fresh look at what it means to be a real man in today's society.

2

The Meaning of Manhood

Since God is far more concerned with the real inner man—the heart—than he is with externals, the next question is, What is a real man anyway? Does he walk or talk or dress in a certain way? Does he only eat red meat or bench press a certain weight? Does he have a certain look about him or a special way with women? Does he hang out with a particular kind of people, pursue a certain kind of career, or worship in a certain kind of church?

The answer differs depending on whether we assess real manhood through our society's eyes or through the eyes of Jesus Christ.

Society's Measure

In our society some confusion exists as to what constitutes a real man. Some years ago, *The 49 Percent Majority: The Male Sex Role* was published. (The title refers to the fact that although men comprise approximately 49 percent of the population, they seem to be clearly in the majority when it comes to such things as economic power and political influence, because ours is a male-dominated society.) Authors Deborah S. David and Robert Brannon point out four themes that seem to define the common conception of masculinity. Let's consider these secular "measures of a man."

First, real men don't do sissy stuff. That means you don't eat dainty or elaborate food or do things traditionally done mostly by women, such as needlepoint (unless you are former football great Rosey Grier; he is big enough to do anything he likes). A real man doesn't indulge in female talk or enjoy female things. Many sociologists think this is related to a latent fear of homosexuality.

Second, according to the authors, a real man needs to be in control. Refusing help of any kind, he rejects and ignores the counsel of others. He views himself as a success and believes the evidence is on every hand. This man expects everybody to recognize him as the "big wheel."

Third, and closely related to the big-wheel syndrome, is the sturdy oak syndrome. It requires the man at all times to be tough, confident, self-reliant, and able to stand firm. He allows everyone else to lean on him because he is the one who will not, under any circumstances, be shaken.

The fourth characteristic is colorfully described as the "give 'em hell" syndrome (forgive the language). A real man must be aggressive, daring, and even violent at times, if the situation requires it. He is highly competitive, and he makes things happen.

To many in our society, David and Brannon's conclusions sum up what they believe are the indisputable facts about real men. However, there is a problem with all of this. Despite all these big wheels and sturdy oaks, men still die at a younger age than women. According to the latest statistics I have seen, they commit 90 percent of all major crimes, are responsible for 99 percent of all rape, and 95 percent of all burglaries. Ninety-four percent of all drunk drivers are men. They also commit 70 percent of all suicides and 91 percent of all offenses against the family.

Evidently, men are not as much in control as we have been led to believe. Things are not going well with these "real men."

During the 1980s, men, sometimes in direct response to the outspoken criticisms of women in general and feminists in particular, did make attempts to get in touch with their "feminine side." In the 1990s, *Iron John* led some men into the woods to beat their chests and their drums in an effort to discover their true manhood. Even more recently, the remarkable phenomenon of Promise Keepers has shown that many modern men are looking for a deeper meaning of masculinity and how it affects their relationships with each other and with women. Time will tell how deeply the male psyche is being touched and changed, but of one thing we can be certain: Change in the right direction, which we will get to shortly, is long overdue.

Jesus' Measure of a Man

No human being can cope with the heavy demands of living up to society's view of true manhood. Its requirements are too burdensome. For that reason it is essential we take a second look at the question, "What is a real man?"

The answer comes loud and clear from Jesus. "Hey! If you want to see a real man, take a look at John the Baptist. There has never been a greater one than John." John had six admirable traits that qualified him as a real man: sincerity, simplicity, conviction, courage, vision, and vulnerability.

Sincerity

John's sincerity was affirmed by the crowds that came to hear him preach. When he spoke, people listened. They found his words so important that they dropped what they were doing and went to hear him. His sincere, straightforward message rang true to their ears.

King Herod, who was eventually responsible for John's death, sent for the Baptist even after he was imprisoned. He loved to listen to John. And even though he wasn't very good at following John's teachings, he was utterly intrigued by the man himself. Herod, himself a despot, recognized in John a real man of integrity.

John's disciples also testified to his sincerity. Even though the Baptist, at the time of his imprisonment, encouraged some of his disciples to leave him and follow Jesus, we know that they visited John at regular intervals. They continued to identify with him—they stuck with him and were interested in and concerned about him. Why? Because of his sincerity that had shown through so clearly.

Simplicity

John's simplicity was clear in his disciplined lifestyle. He ate locusts and wild honey, and wore a garment of camel's hair with a rope around his waist. He lived in the wilderness. Of course I am not suggesting that being a real man means you have to risk getting stung for your supper! But I am saying that John was disciplined. He was a man of prayer, a man who fasted, a man of simple tastes. Like Jesus, he was not concerned about fine clothes and luxuries. His simple approach to life was exhibited by a disciplined lifestyle—something worth imitating in these days of affluence and waste.

The simplicity of John's life mirrored the directness of his message. He proclaimed that the kingdom of God was at hand and warned people not to waste their time on anything else until they had prepared for it. He was a simple, direct man who cut through the frills and froth to get down to the real issues. The world needs men who will say, "Listen, people, the kingdom of God is at hand! Shape up!"

The simplicity of John's message is further illustrated by the way he presented Jesus as the king of the kingdom. He came straight to the point: "There is one coming after me who is preferred before me, the one to whom we look. I'm not the important one. It is he who is all important" (see John 1:29-31). He understood the supreme importance of the kingdom and was unequivocal about the greatness of the king. He presented his truth to the people and called them to repentance, confession, and commitment. Converted people were expected to demonstrate the change in their lives by a completely different attitude toward God and life itself. This is simple, straightforward stuff.

Conviction

Another of John's characteristics was his strong sense of conviction. This was particularly evident in seven areas.

Reality. Symbolism was common in the society of John's day. He was involved in some of it himself—the very fact that his name was based on the symbol of baptism suggests as much. When he required the people to confess their sin and repent of it, he demanded that they show some evidence of repentance. One of the ways they did this was by being symbolically baptized in water. "But," John said, "don't be confused. I baptize you with water, but the one who is coming after me will baptize you with the Holy Spirit and with fire" (see Luke 3:16-17). He was implying that while our symbolic acts are important, the crux of the matter is the attitude of the heart—that's reality.

Hypocrisy. John confronted the Pharisees, Sadducees, and other hypocrites who came to him: "You generation of vipers, what are you doing here? You snakes!" That's a real man, according to Jesus. John was totally frank with them because he recognized their hypocrisy, play-acting, and preoccupation with externals. Out of deep conviction, he repudiated their apathy about their failure to repent, confess, and undergo a complete change in their lives.

Integrity. Jesus himself took note of John's integrity. In Luke 7:24-28 he said, in effect, "What did you folks expect to see when you went out to the Jordan or into the wilderness to hear John the Baptist speak? A reed blowing gently in the breeze, swayed by this opinion and that? One who wouldn't ruffle the water or rock the boat? Or did you go to see a man dressed in fine clothes, enjoying the very best of everything and living high on the hog? Well, you were surprised, weren't you? Because John wasn't concerned about fine clothes and he wasn't a reed swayed by every breeze of opinion. Instead, you found that John was committed to integrity, righteousness, and truth—qualities of a real man."

Purity. Perhaps the best way to illustrate this is to recall John the Baptist's interaction with King Herod and his wife, Herodias. One day John talked to Herod while his wife was present, and what he had to say did not sit well with Herodias.

John said, "King Herod, your marriage to Herodias is not right. Herodias was married to your brother Philip, but you and Herodias went to Rome and had an affair. You broke up your brother's marriage, you got a divorce, and then went through with this improper new marriage. It is not right, and I'm telling you so to your face."

John was utterly convinced that Herod's lifestyle and the sensuality of his court were wrong. Morality and purity were important to John. This brings us to another of John's characteristics.

Courage. Because John had convictions about reality, hypocrisy, integrity, and purity, he had the courage to speak out against the immorality of Herod and Herodias. He allowed his convictions to govern his actions and he dared to challenge evil and evildoers. He believed that evil needs to be exposed and good needs to be encouraged. It takes courage to confront evil wherever it appears, whether in the workplace, the classroom, or a relationship. It takes courage to confront it in our children, in our social circles, and among our friends. But that is what real men do.

Because of his courage and conviction, John dared to confront evil in high places. But he also endorsed what was good. It is one thing to knock evil; it is an entirely different matter to forthrightly proclaim what is good. John was deeply committed to the teaching of righteousness; he was able to digest these teachings and apply them to the society of his day.

Vision. John was a man with a vision. In describing him, Jesus had asked, "What did you expect to see? A reed blowing in the wind or a man dressed in fine clothing? No, you went to see a prophet. And that is exactly what you got."

What is a prophet? In Jesus' day a prophet was also called a seer—one who sees. A seer looks beyond the immediate to the ultimate. He has been given the perspective of God himself and is able to see the meaning behind events. A seer has a vision for possibilities. He or she looks through the situation and envisions how it can glorify God, looking past people's exterior to discover what really makes them tick. The true seer can concentrate on the issues that determine whether we actually are good or evil. This was the vision of John the Baptist, and it must be the vision of anyone who claims to be a real man today.

Vulnerability. John's vulnerability came to light during a very important experience in his life—his imprisonment after he had confronted Herod and Herodias. As he sat in his cell, his disciples visited, bringing reports of what Jesus was saying and doing. John then began to doubt his calling and wonder if he had been mistaken. So he asked his disciples, "Would you go back to Jesus and ask him a question for me? Would you ask him if he is really the Messiah? Is he really the one we are looking for, or are we looking for another?"

What an interesting insight this gives us into the mind of John the Baptist. In his doubt, he reveals a winsome vulnerability. According to research, the five most difficult statements for the modern man to make are (1) I don't know, (2) I was wrong, (3) I need help, (4) I'm afraid, and (5) I'm sorry. In other words, according to the world's definition, real men do not show vulnerability. If they do, their masculinity is in question. But John was not afraid to admit his vulnerability.

In my opinion, our culture has very carefully programmed men not to be vulnerable. We're supposed to hide our feelings, not come to grips with who we really are, and not be honest about ourselves. We can laugh about men who are afraid even to admit that they need directions, but I believe that a contributing factor to many of our society's ills is its false conception of masculinity. A real man demonstrates sincerity and simplicity, courage and conviction, vision and vulnerability. He can look directly at others and say, "I don't know" or "I might have been wrong" or "I'm afraid" or "I need help" or "I'm sorry." That is vulnerability!

There is a marked difference between this kind of humble vulnerability and some of the modern variations on the vulnerable theme. True vulnerability is not about the endless soul-searching of those who appear addicted to a therapeutic method whereby they constantly explore their feelings. It does not recast men as victims. Once the mind is set in the victim mode it is well nigh impossible for people—men or women—to see themselves objectively as divinely created, divinely loved but desperately sinful people.

John the Baptist's vulnerability is shown in two ways—his honesty and his humility. His humility is unbelievable. One of his best known statements was in reference to Jesus: "He must become greater; I must become less" (John 3:30). Do you remember the circumstances? John was a prophet, and the crowds had been flocking to hear him. Then some people said to him, "Don't you realize that the crowds are rushing to see Jesus?"

He said, "Sure, I realize that. I sent some of them over myself, because I must go on decreasing. Jesus is the one who must go on increasing." There is nothing phony about John's humility. He has come to grips with who he really is in relation to Jesus.

Various symbols illustrate the relationship between Jesus and John the Baptist. Jesus was the Light; John the Baptist was the lamp. John was the medium through whom Jesus did his work. On one occasion, John said to his disciples as Jesus walked past, "Look, the Lamb of God, who takes away the sin of the world!" (John 1:29). Jesus was the Way; John the Baptist was the signpost. Jesus was the Message; John was the messenger. Jesus was the Word; John was the voice.

John didn't like to talk about himself. His main concern was to understand himself in the light of who Jesus Christ is. When we come to terms with who we are compared to Jesus Christ, we find it's not too difficult to be humble.

John's vulnerability was also reflected in his honesty. He was honest about his doubts as he sat in his prison cell. Why did he wonder if Jesus really was the Messiah? He must have thought, "If Jesus is the Messiah, why doesn't he get me out of this place? The Messiah is supposed to release the captives, isn't he?" John was honest about his doubts and fears.

We follow all kinds of models today, whether they be successful CEOs, self-help or motivational gurus, sports celebrities, actors, or rock stars. They may or may not have qualities that we admire. We can't go wrong, however, if we select a model who had the imprimatur of Jesus: John the Baptist. Jesus said there was not a greater man born of woman.

An enigmatic phrase concludes Jesus' statement about John. "Among those born of women there is no one greater than John; yet the one who is least in the kingdom of God is greater than he" (Luke 7:28). Even "the least in the kingdom" is greater than he? What does Jesus mean? He seems to be saying, "Look at all the qualities of manhood and remember that these are only secondary. The primary objective is to make sure you are part of the kingdom."

One could exhibit all the greatest male characteristics in the world and still miss the kingdom. A real man is part of the kingdom and acknowledges the King. He has come to repentance, is open to confession, and proves the reality of his repentance by his converted lifestyle. In the chapters that follow we will look at some of the characteristics of that converted lifestyle, as well as the ways those traits affect the roles men take in modern society.

VALUES OF A
CHRISTIAN MAN

For you were once darkness, but now you are light in the Lord. Live as children of light (for the fruit of the light consists in all goodness, righteousness and truth) and find out what pleases the Lord. Have nothing to do with the fruitless deeds of darkness, but rather expose them. For it is shameful even to mention what the disobedient do in secret. But everything exposed by the light becomes visible, for it is light that makes everything visible. This is why it is said: "Wake up, O sleeper, rise from the dead, and Christ will shine on you." Be very careful, then, how you live—not as unwise but as wise, making the most of every opportunity, because the days are evil. Therefore do not be foolish, but understand what the Lord's will is.

Ephesians 5:8-17

❖❖❖

3

Faithfulness: Following the Will of God

If I were to compile a Top Ten list of subjects people bring up in pastoral counseling sessions, questions about God's will would hover close to Number 1. All Christians, men and women alike, are concerned about God's will for their lives. But I've found that men tend to worry about it more than women. Perhaps men still feel the traditional burden of being the breadwinner and worry more about finding the right career. Or maybe it's a built-in spirit of adventure and discovery. Possibly some may have the mistaken notion that their life calling is more important than that of their wife or of women in general. Most certainly it is not.

Looking at the book of Ephesians, we can gather three main ideas about God's will: It is purposeful, personal, and practical.

Lives of Purpose

Two important phrases occur at the beginning of this epistle. First, "He chose us in him *before the creation of the world* to be holy and blameless in his sight. In love he predestined us to be adopted as his sons through Jesus Christ" (Eph. 1:4-5, italics added). This is a statement about God's purpose for his people, a purpose that was set in motion "before the creation of the world." Keep that in the back of your mind as we move on.

The second phrase occurs a few verses later: "He made known to us the mystery of his will according to his good pleasure, which he purposed in Christ, to be put into effect *when the times will have reached their fulfillment*" (1:9-10, italics added). Put simply, God's purposes stretch from eternity to eternity. Why is this so important? If we recognize that there is an eternal God who is working out his eternal purposes, and that his purposes will not be thwarted, then our whole life will be affected.

Everybody has a world view or a concept of history. Some say the world lurches from one set of circumstances to another, that it is inherently meaningless and absurd. Others say that history rests in the hands of human beings, who alone will determine its outcome. Still others say that history is cyclical and that our lives are merely reincarnations of a previous life. The Christian, however, sees his life as part of God's sovereign purpose, one that has originated in eternity and will be consummated in eternity. That makes a difference in the way we live.

It also is important that God's purposes are centered in Christ. At the end of verse 10, Paul wrote, "to bring all things in heaven and on earth together under one head, *even Christ*" (italics aded). God's eternal purposes find their consummation in Christ—in his cosmic lordship, in his transcendent majesty, and in his ultimate authority. What is the world coming to? Inevitably and inextricably, it is coming to the point where everything comes under the headship of Christ.

If all this sounds too grandiose and mystical and unreal, in the middle of this vast statement, the apostle Paul talks about God's purposes for individuals. For instance, he begins his letter with these words: "Paul, an apostle of Christ Jesus by the will of God." God's sovereign purpose has an individual application. He wants Paul to be an apostle, and Paul knows this. He understands God's will for his life.

That may be great for Paul, but what about the rest of us? Look at verses 4 and 5: "He chose us in him before the creation of the world to be holy and blameless in his sight. In love he predestined us to be adopted as his sons through Jesus Christ." Now Paul is speaking not just about himself, but about the Ephesians. And if we believe that these truths apply to God's people at all times, we can reasonably infer that God has predestined and chosen something for us today as well.

God's Personal Plan

God's will is not only purposeful, it is personal. In Ephesians 2:8-9, Paul wrote, "For it is by grace you have been saved, through faith—and this not from yourselves, it is the gift of God—not by works, so that no one can boast." One of the hardest things to do in western Christianized society is to persuade people that they don't get to heaven by being good. They find the idea offensive. Yet the Bible states it over and over again: We are not saved by our works.

Does that mean we can lean back and say, "I'll just relax and do whatever I want"? No, because now we come to a lesser-known verse, Ephesians 2:10: "For we are God's workmanship, created in Christ Jesus to do good works, which God prepared in advance for us to do." Having made it clear that we are not saved by our good works, Paul makes it clear that we are saved *for* good works.

The word translated *workmanship* here is similar to the English word *poem*. It means literally that we are God's work of art, his masterpiece. Whenever I preach, I feel so fortunate, because I'm standing before a roomful of divine masterpieces. Those in my congregation and you who are reading this book are all works of art—assuming, of course, you've been saved by grace through faith.

Why did God take all this trouble to create these works of art? Because he has a plan in place and it relates to us. God has good works set out for us to do. What sort of good works? Paul gives us an idea in 1 Thessalonians 4:3: "It is God's will that you should be sanctified"—that is, holy.

From time to time people come to me for advice in dealing with a problem, and I'm more than happy to help. But occasionally somebody comes in and says, "Stuart, I don't have a problem. I just need some help discovering God's will. Can you help me?"

"Oh sure, that's easy," I reply. Usually they're surprised. But how can anyone be confused about God's will with verses like this: "It is God's will that you should be sanctified"?

Let me be more specific about this, just as Paul was. "It is God's will that you should be sanctified, that you should avoid sexual immorality; that each of you should learn to control his own body in a way that is holy and honorable, not in passionate lust like the heathen" (4:3-5). What does it mean to be holy? It means to recognize that there are forces at work in you—passions, lusts, desires, aspirations, needs, longings—that need to be controlled. Some people have a great deal of sexual desire; when they don't control it, they fall into sexual immorality. Others may have a greed problem or a money problem or an anger problem instead. It doesn't matter what the desires and longings are; if they are not controlled, they may become partly or even totally illegitimate. People who allow that to happen are not living holy lives.

Now look at what Paul says in verse 8: "He who rejects this instruction does not reject man but God, who gives you his Holy Spirit." He says that because the only way you and I can cope with these desires is to control our bodies by the Spirit whom God gives to us. A holy life is a disciplined life—disciplined in the power of the Spirit. That is the lifestyle God wills for his people.

Consider 1 Thessalonians 5:16-17: "Be joyful always; pray continually; give thanks in all circumstances, for this is God's will for you in Christ Jesus." This verse moves us from a discussion of lifestyle in general to our specific attitudes. It is God's will that a Christian world view should lead to developing a certain kind of lifestyle in the power of the Spirit. That lifestyle should show itself in certain attitudes.

Attitude is ninety percent of the battle. Some people are very gifted and highly trained, but because they have rotten attitudes they give others nothing but headaches. Others may be less gifted or not as well trained, but their superb attitude makes them a joy to be around. If you are really lucky, you have the opportunity to work with people who are highly gifted, thoroughly trained, *and* have a wonderful attitude. Can you imagine what it would be like to spend your days with a joyful, thankful, prayerful person? Can you picture yourself *being* such a person? That is God's will for you and me.

A Practical Plan

Finally, God's will is not only purposeful and personal, it is also practical. That means we can discover his will and that we can do it.

However, when it comes to discovering God's will for our lives, we often get hung up on one point of confusion. I want to clear that up before proceeding.

Gary Friesen and J. Robin Maxson wrote a controversial but helpful book entitled *Decision Making and the Will of God.* They explain that traditionally Christians have viewed God's will as having three parts: his *sovereign* will (from eternity to eternity he will work out his purposes and nobody will stop him); his *moral* will (that we should live a holy life and have a joyful, thankful, and prayerful attitude); and his *individual* will (where you go to school, which major you choose, who you marry, where you live, what kind of job you get). This view makes it appear that God is equally concerned about all three areas.

A problem arises, though, when we try to determine God's individual will. Friesen and Maxson illustrate the dilemma by drawing a big circle representing God's sovereign and moral will; inside it they draw a tiny little dot which is God's individual will. According to the traditional view, in order to be "in" the will of God, you have to hit the dot. Unfortunately, people get themselves into a total tizzy trying to hit that dot. Some try very earnestly and prayerfully to hit it, while others give up altogether, believing it to be an impossible task.

I have found that many people picture God's will as a high wire at the circus, where you climb to a great height and, while the crowds below watch and hold their breath, you slowly, carefully, inch your way across, knowing that if you make one slip, it is all over. That's how many Christians are moving through their lives. Either they teeter on the wire in terror, or they safely stay put, observing but never acting. This approach to God's will makes it easy to become totally paralyzed.

Friesen and Maxson address this problem with the controversial notion that God does not have an individual will for you. In other words, there is no dot that you must hit, no high wire you might fall off. As long as you remain within the circle of God's sovereign and moral will, then you are free to make your own choices. I am not sure I completely agree with them, but I am pretty close to their position.

I would suggest that God's will is not a high wire—it is more like a six-lane highway. God knows where you are and he knows where he wants you to go, but he leaves you some options. You can drive in the fast or the slow lane, pull off when you need to rest or refuel, but you are still traveling in the direction God wants you to go. I realize that may sound controversial, but it takes away the paralyzing concept that you have got to hit a dot or keep both feet exactly on a wire. If you truly believe God is concerned about such detail, where do you draw the line? Does God really care if I wear a red or a blue tie today? Does it matter to him whether I eat Wheaties or Cheerios for breakfast? That's why I think a broader view of God's will is prudent.

Having said that, let me give you a couple of ideas to ponder as you try to discover God's will for you. One is to make sure that you have the deep desire to do his will. Paul puts it this way in Ephesians 5:10: "Find out what pleases the Lord." Some people only care about pleasing themselves, while others worry about pleasing everybody else.

The Christian man tries to find out what pleases the Lord. Of course it is not necessarily wrong to please yourself or others, but our overriding desire in life should be to please our Lord.

Once you have that kind of heartfelt desire, then dedicate yourself to acting on it. In Romans 12:1-2, Paul writes, "Therefore, I urge you, brothers, in view of God's mercy, to offer your bodies as living sacrifices, holy and pleasing to God—this is your spiritual act of worship. Do not conform any longer to the pattern of this world, but be transformed by the renewing of your mind. Then you will be able to test and approve what God's will is—his good, pleasing and perfect will." We dedicate ourselves by regularly saying to God, "Lord, I present my body to you for your service, to be what you want me to be, and to do what you want me to do. I realize that my life is easily conformed to secularized thought patterns, but I don't want that. I want my mind renewed so that I can conform to your principles. So I dedicate my body, my mind, my self, to finding out what pleases you and then doing it." As we do this, Scripture says, we will prove God's will to be good and perfect and acceptable.

Many people want to find out where God's road leads, but they haven't shown a fundamental desire to do God's will. And they haven't dedicated themselves wholeheartedly to it. Why? Maybe they have underlined in their Bibles that God's will is good and perfect and acceptable, but they have yet to underline it in their hearts. Instead, they hold on to a nasty suspicion that God's will is not so good and acceptable, that it will somehow be boring or unpleasant or painful. In other words, they really do not want to do God's will. Therein lies the problem. I am absolutely convinced that when Christians begin to develop a deep desire and a heartfelt dedication to the Lord, they begin to discover his plans of glory. You don't need to be looking for tiny dots, or perching precariously on high wires. Just nurture that deep desire and that dedication, and God will lead you down the right path. There is freedom, joy, and even delight in this approach to life.

I said above that not only can God's will be discovered, it can be done. Consider the closing verses of the letter to the Hebrews: "May the God of peace . . . equip you with everything good for doing his will, and may he work in us what is pleasing to him" (13:20-21). These verses remind us that God gives us everything we need for doing his will as we allow his Spirit to work in us. He doesn't say, "OK, this is what will please me—now go do it." He says, "This is what will please me, and my Spirit will empower you to do it." In his strength, we can do anything he asks of us.

When we take these steps and live by these principles, we'll not only discover God's will, but we will also see just how desirable his will is. Our lives will begin to glorify God and contribute to his kingdom. We will begin to notice, with Paul, that our lives are characterized by that which is good and right and true (Eph. 5:9). That is what God's purpose is all about. So don't be foolish, men. Understand God's will. Discover it through your own deep desire and dedication. And remain faithful to it all your life.

As God works in you and opens the way for you, you will find that you delight in doing his will. In addition, you will find yourself transformed into the kind of man God wants you to be. Not only will your passions and desires be under his control, but your priorities will become God's priorities, reflecting the Lord's perspective on what is important—and what is not so important—in this life. And righteous priorities are a key value of a Christian man.

4

Focus: Making God Our First Priority

In the Sermon on the Mount, Jesus calls his followers to live a lifestyle guided by a distinctive philosophy rooted in the eternal Word of God. Not that surprisingly, it is a lifestyle often at odds with the world around us. One of the tensions we encounter as Christian men is being constantly bombarded by philosophies totally opposed to biblical truth. And one of our biggest struggles in this topsy-turvy world is to establish and remain true to our Christian priorities—to be focused on God.

Discovering Our Priorities

We have all been encouraged to "put first things first." The problem is discovering what those first things are. All kinds of demands are placed on Christian men. It's relatively easy to say, "Major on the major, and minor on the minor"—but the difficulty lies in determining what is minor. It involves constant re-evaluation.

Personally, I have a real problem establishing priorities. Not that there is any lack of advice from others. Some people in my church have been concerned for my physical welfare, encouraging me to make physical fitness a priority. Some were concerned about my prayer life; they had been reading about Martin Luther, who spent several hours at prayer in the early hours of the day, and they wondered how I fared in that regard! Others worried that I might be neglecting my own family because of my devotion to the people in the church. Another person, concerned that I remain in touch with what is going on in the world around me, gave me a book club membership.

There are other pressures on me as a pastor. Some people think I am away from my pulpit too much—away from my church family. On the other hand, I have a stack of mail inviting me to speak here and speak there, wonderful opportunities to minister the Word. What do I do? How do I arrive at the proper priorities? How do I keep from neglecting my work at home as I respond to these opportunities away from home?

Some people are well-organized when it comes to establishing priorities. They make a list and carry out each task one, two, three. Perhaps you are that kind of person. I can make a list without any trouble—then I lose it! Clearly, we all have different abilities when it comes to prioritizing. For that reason, I believe the real solution lies outside ourselves, in the Word of God. When Jesus talks about our priorities, he focuses on three areas of our lives: our activities, our anxieties, and our ambitions.

In the Sermon on the Mount, Jesus says, "Do not store up for yourselves treasures on earth" (Matt. 6:19). There is no better way to measure our priorities than to look at our activities. Our activities translate into priorities; where we spend our time is a good indicator of what is already important to us. The old saying, "We can always find time to do what we really want to do" is partly true. There are certain things we must do, but after they are done we have discretionary time left over. What we do then is a measure of our priorities.

Our anxieties are also a gauge of our priorities. In verse 25 Jesus says, "Therefore I tell you, do not worry about your life, what you will eat or drink; or about your body, what you will wear." We all have anxieties, and Jesus touches on most of them here—finances, food, fashion, fitness, and the future. Whatever I am anxious about takes priority in my life.

The word *seek* in Matthew 6 gives us a clue to our ambitions, a third indicator of our priorities: "For the pagans run after all these things, and your heavenly Father knows that you need them. But seek first his kingdom and his righteousness, and all these things will be given to you as well" (vv. 32-33). The word *seek* conveys the idea of desire, intense ambition, and endeavor. When Jesus talks about what people are seeking for or running after, he is talking about their ambitions. Egocentric ambition can ruin a person—but lack of ambition can be just as disastrous.

Now that we have three accurate means for gauging our priorities, the next step is to determine what they are telling us, what our priorities really are.

Rating Our Priorities

Jesus addressed priorities in Matthew 6:19-20 when he said, "Do not store up for yourselves treasures on earth, where moth and rust destroy, and where thieves break in and steal. But store up for yourselves treasures in heaven, where moth and rust do not destroy, and where thieves do not break in and steal." Jesus was saying, Measure your activities in the light of eternity. Use your God-given raw materials—your strength, skills, time, and energy—according to priorities set forth by God himself.

It is easy to devote ourselves to activities not remotely related to eternity. We can live our earthly lives without storing up any heavenly treasure whatsoever. And when we leave the earthly treasure we have amassed, what happens? It remains for the moths and rust to feed upon. And when we reach our heavenly destination, we will have nothing there—we will be destitute.

I am not suggesting that secular work—working in a bank, say—is wrong. I am saying that what we must do, regardless of our type of activity, is perform our tasks in light of eternity. It is possible to be deeply involved in all kinds of activities without giving a thought to God at all. It is also possible to be involved in seemingly secular duties during which we are constantly driven by a desire to live out God's will.

Another way to rate our priorities is to evaluate our anxieties. In verse 32 Jesus urges us to look at our needs from God's perspective, realizing that he can and will supply all our needs according to his riches in glory. Our lifestyles and our priorities are determined by our attitude toward God's ability to supply our needs. I must live my life in the light of one tremendous fact: My heavenly Father knows my needs and is abundantly able to meet them. If I am anxious about many things, I will miss my Father's best for me. Rating my anxieties will show me clearly whether I trust in the providence of God—his ability to care for me.

Jesus tells us in verse 33 that our ambition should be to

"seek . . . first the kingdom of God" (KJV). What a superb statement! But how many of us can say unequivocally that we know exactly what it means to seek God's kingdom?

The Kingdom of God

There are three things about the kingdom of God we must recognize. First, it must be *experienced.* In John 3 we meet a man called Nicodemus, a ruler of the Jews, highly articulate, well educated. Nicodemus had heard of this young carpenter who came from Nazareth, and he was interested in what Jesus had to say. He even called Jesus "Rabbi" (John 3:2), a title of respect.

When he at last sits down with Nicodemus, Jesus gets right to the root of the ruler's problem: "I tell you the truth, no one can see the kingdom of God unless he is born again" (John 3:3, TEV). Jesus' statement was not just for Nicodemus; it applies to everyone today as well. In order to experience the kingdom of God, we must be born again. On the authority of the Word of God, if I have not been born again, I cannot be a member of the kingdom of God. This must come first if our priorities are going to be in line with God's plan.

Being born again applies to our ambitions as well. If my goal in life is to be born again, then I will not get hung up on lesser things like making lots of money and ascending the corporate ladder. If becoming a member of God's kingdom is my first priority, other aspects of my life will fall into proper perspective.

Once the kingdom of God has been experienced, it must then be *expressed.* Paul writes about this in 1 Corinthians 4:19-20: "But I will come to you very soon, if the Lord is

47

willing, and then I will find out not only how these arrogant people are talking, but what power they have. For the kingdom of God is not a matter of talk but of power."

To paraphrase the apostle, the kingdom of God is dynamite! It is not some nebulous "something" waiting in the future somewhere. It is powerfully alive in the here and now. Therefore my priority must be to demonstrate the power of God here and now. I must not be swept up in the secular thinking around me. I must not be swallowed up by the false ambitions of my contemporaries who surround me. Rather, I must be totally involved in the kingdom. That is the message Jesus is conveying here. If my first priority is to survive in the business world or to be successful socially, then I may miss the kingdom.

The kingdom must be experienced and expressed. But it must also be *expanded.* "And this gospel of the kingdom will be preached in the whole world as a testimony to all nations, and then the end will come" (Matt. 24:14). Any man who understands the commitment of Jesus Christ to establish his kingdom in the lives of people from every tribe and tongue and nation should recognize that he has a part to play in this extension ministry. It will become a priority.

If the kingdom is first in our lives, that will mean experiencing, expressing, and expanding it will govern our priorities in life.

Relating Our Priorities

Jesus told us that our concern should not be for earthly treasure, but for treasure of the heavenly kind. Fine. Are my financial priorities earthly or heavenly? How do I handle my paycheck? Have I written across it, "First the kingdom"? My checks have pictures on them—perhaps yours do too. Wouldn't it be great if our checks could have a picture of heaven on them, to remind us to put the kingdom first? Or what if they could have pictures of hungry people on them? That would remind us of God's priorities in terms of our finances.

First the kingdom. That means I am going to apply eternal concepts to earthly affairs and activities. If I am going to be a Christian man and invest my time, strength, and energy for eternity, I may have to view certain activities not in terms of what is wrong with them, but in terms of "What is the point?" It is not enough merely to say they are not harming anyone. Instead, I must ask myself, "What good am I doing? What am I accomplishing?" This is applying the concept of the eternal to the earthly.

In my activities, anxieties, and ambitions, do I have an overriding concern that the kingdom of God be experienced by all kinds of people, starting with my own family? Above all other concerns, do I desire that his kingdom be extended? Is that the way my priorities are arranged? If that's the case, I will have obeyed Jesus' admonition to seek first the kingdom of God.

Christian men cannot be content to settle for anything less. Our spiritual lives depend on our focus on this purpose. In the next chapter we will look at how solid, biblical priorities are crucial if we are to remain strong despite challenging circumstances and constant temptations.

Blessed is the man who perseveres under trial,
because when he has stood the test, he will
receive the crown of life that God has promised
to those who love him.

James 1:12

5

Fortitude: Standing Up to Temptation

We sometimes facetiously say, "I can resist anything but temptation." That is cute, but when we look squarely at the problems people have in their lives, society's ills, and the countless wrongs people do to other people, we see that behind so many of those problems are temptations that were mishandled.

I don't think anyone would deny that temptation is real. Some might say, though, that it is not real important. "Sure, I get tempted," they admit, "but so what? I kind of like it and sometimes I give in to it, but I don't worry too much about it." Or, "Yes, I get tempted, but show me somebody who doesn't. I'm just like everyone else, and there's nothing I can do about it." Still others say, "Frankly, I love dabbling in forbidden territory—it adds spice to an otherwise boring life."

On the other hand, most Christian men who take their faith seriously are concerned about temptation and how to deal with it appropriately. They recognize areas of their lives in which they are not handling temptation adequately, and they want biblical guidance.

A Correct Perspective

The opening verses of the epistle of James offer insight into the nature of temptation and our response to it. But before we can approach it, we need to gain a correct perspective on temptation. The Greek word James uses here can mean "testing" or "trial," or it can mean "temptation." Clearly there's a connection between a testing and a temptation, but they are not the same. This is how to tell the difference: A testing gives you the opportunity to do something right; a temptation is designed to entice you to do something wrong.

Unfortunately, we do not always know ahead of time which one we are experiencing. At any given moment, any set of circumstances may present us with the option to do right or wrong. If we do right, the experience is beneficial to us and our faith is strengthened. We have been tested and have grown from the experience. But if we choose to do wrong, we have allowed the situation to become a temptation that could have serious consequences. This is the double-edged sense in which James uses the word for "testing" or "temptation."

The second aspect of a correct perspective on temptation is realizing that overcoming temptation involves blessing. James writes, "Blessed is the man who perseveres under trial, because when he has stood the test, he will receive the crown of life that God has promised to those who love him" (1:12). Pressures, he is saying, are going to come our way, but they are entering our lives so that we might persevere. Bright prospects lie ahead for those who persevere under pressure. Even though we may be battered, bloodied, and bruised from the road we have traveled, when we arrive in God's presence having persevered, we will receive the "crown of life," that is, eternal life.

"Do you mean I have to wait until I get to heaven to get the crown of life eternal?" some bright Bible student may say. Well, yes and no. Yes, in the sense that you enter into the practical experience of eternal life only when you move out of time into eternity. No, in the sense that Scripture teaches that we can have the assurance of eternal life—and a taste of what heaven will be like—while we are still here on earth.

We can be certain of these bright prospects of perseverance based on two phrases in verse 12. The first phrase mentions the crown of life "that God has promised." God cannot lie or deny himself. He is faithful to his word, and anything he promises can be counted on absolutely. God does not need to promise us a thing. When he does, he stakes his reputation on that promise. He stands behind it with all of his being.

The second phrase mentions that God promised the crown of life "to those who love him." People have all kinds of theories about who is going to receive eternal life. But Scripture is straightforward: Those who love God will receive the crown of life after they have persevered. The Bible says that we love God because he first loved us. Loving God is our response to his grace, to his care and his loving generosity. When I become aware of my lost condition and I realize God loves me anyway, I love him in return. When I realize I cannot save myself, and that God sent Christ to die in my place, I love him. When I realize that God has promised me eternal life, I love him. And when I realize that God offers all that I need to live a life that pleases him, I love him. Therein lies the blessednessof the man under pressure.

James is not introducing a new theme here. He is simply expanding on what he said in verse 2: "Consider it pure joy, my brothers, whenever you face trials of many kinds." Why? Because testings allow you to see how strong your faith is. They allow you to mature, to develop your spiritual muscles, as an athlete works his bodily muscles in order to build strength and endurance. Testing—making the right choices when faced with temptations—builds stronger, more faithful Christian men.

A Clear Perception

If we are going to have a clear perception of temptation, we need to refute several standard theories about it. One is that temptation is all God's fault: "Sure, I've done wrong things, but that's the way God made me and there's nothing I can do about it. How can he judge me for doing what he made me do anyway?"

Here is another one. Do you remember the seventies comedian Flip Wilson? He certainly had a distinctive theology. His alterego was a woman named Geraldine. Whenever Geraldine did something bad, she would always say, "The *devil* made me do it!" Wouldn't it be great to fall back on Flip Wilson's theology whenever we mess up? It really gets us off the hook. "Hey God," we can say, "you know there is a big nasty devil out there and I'm no match for him. He's smart and I'm dumb. So don't blame me or hold me accountable—the devil made me do it."

Then there is the temptation theory first used by Adam and relied upon by men ever since. When Adam got himself into trouble and the Lord asked him, "Why did you do what you did?" Adam blamed Eve, the woman God had created for his companionship. There is no shortage of men who blame their problems on the women in their life. But Adam didn't stop there—he took it one step further: the woman *you gave me,* he said. "Now God, let's get this clear," he was saying. "You made Eve and you brought her to me. It's really your fault."

Others take a different approach: "My parents made me do it." They might not say this overtly, but the attitude comes through. For example, it is common for people who are struggling with a problem or a personal crisis to enlist the help of a therapist. Frequently the therapy focuses on childhood and the upbringing that may have contributed to the problem. Unfortunately, many people draw the wrong conclusion from such analysis, thinking, "Aha! It's all my parents' fault! I'm not responsible for what happened— they are. I'm just a victim of circumstances."

All of these theories on temptation, along with other variations, echo a similar theme: I am not responsible, I am not accountable, I am the victim. Christian men must wholeheartedly reject these attitudes.

In contrast, James presents us with certain truths that must be respected if we are to have a clear perception of temptation. In verse 13 he says, "When tempted, no one should say, 'God is tempting me.' For God cannot be tempted by evil, nor does he tempt anyone." Temptation starts with something inside us known as desire. Some of our desires are evil. James is telling us that there is something within the human heart that is fundamentally antagonistic to God, that has fundamentally rejected God's way of doing things. Call it what you will—sin, evil desire, sin dwelling in you, whatever—it rebels against God's truth and strives for its own way.

Let me offer two scenes for example. After church one Sunday, someone from my congregation goes out to his car and sees a hundred dollar bill on the blacktop. He glances around and, seeing that the coast is clear, deftly scoops it up, leaps into his car, and takes off. Second scene: Same church, same blacktop, same hundred dollar bill, but a different person. This guy thinks, *Oh no, somebody has lost a hundred dollar bill! They are really going to be upset. Maybe if I take it inside they can announce that a sum of money has been found and see if it belongs to anyone.*

See my point? The circumstances are identical, but one person sees an opportunity to do right, while the other feels the urge to do wrong. The difference is the heart. According to Scripture, there is within us an evil desire that can respond to a testing in an inappropriate way. When that evil desire acts, it changes that harmless testing into a dangerous temptation.

Tangled and Hooked

Some commentators think the two Greek words James uses in verse 14 to describe desire come straight out of fishing vocabulary. One means to be entangled in a net; the other means to be hooked. Probably all men can respond to these images by saying, "I know exactly what you mean, James. There are certain areas of my life in which I find myself entangled in wrong desires, and when this happens and I'm not careful, I'm hooked."

James goes on to say that after desire has conceived it gives birth to sin. When the evil desire within me decides to do what is wrong, the decision is sin. The next phrase in verse 15 is striking: "And sin, when it is full-grown, gives birth to death." What a graphic expression! James is saying there will be physical death as a consequence of sin. But he is also warning of a more immediate, spiritual death—that is, spiritual separation from God now. And if we give our entire lives over to temptation, we could even experience a third kind of death, eternal separation from God.

In other words, James is telling us that we must understand the phenomenal impact of temptation. When we allow temptation to take over, our evil desire makes wrong decisions that produce sin. Sin always has a deteriorating, disintegrating effect on our lives. Before long we will find ourselves going the way of death. Yes, we can jokingly say, "I can resist everything but temptation." Or we can treat temptation with the seriousness it deserves by trying to get a correct perspective and a clear perception of it.

Truths about God

Now that we have identified some truths about temptation, it is time to consider some facts about God—his character, his changelessness, and his choice. Look once more at what James writes in verse 13: "When tempted, no one should say, 'God is tempting me.' For God cannot be tempted by evil, nor does he tempt anyone." Notice two things about God's character: There is no trace of evil in him, and it is impossible for him to produce evil. He is intrinsically good, utterly separate from anything that is evil. Evil neither resides in nor emanates from him.

But can it really be true that God does not tempt anyone? After all, the Old Testament is full of situations where God tested people. But remember the double-edged usage of the word mentioned above. While God will allow all kinds of testings to come into our lives in order to produce benevolent results, he would never bring anything into our lives with the intention of producing evil consequences.

"Don't be deceived," James writes in verses 16 and 17, "Every good and perfect gift is from above, coming down from the Father of the heavenly lights, who does not change like shifting shadows." The moon and the stars will change but God never will. He is changeless. He can be counted on to give every good and perfect gift we could ever need to handle the testings that come our way.

Next James speaks of God's choice. "He chose to give us birth through the word of truth, that we might be a kind of firstfruits of all he created" (1:18). We often talk about the day we received Christ or responded to the gospel message, and that's good. But even more significant than the day I responded to God was the day God chose to call me to himself. This good and all-powerful God chose to offer salvation to us. He determined that he wanted us in his presence, and he offered Christ as the basis of our salvation. All of this was his choice.

As we begin to understand God's character, his changelessness, and his choice to work in our lives, our confidence in him will grow dramatically. As that confidence builds up, we will find it easier to trust him in the midst of the testing times. And our trust in him will be greater than the temptation to succumb to the evil.

Truth about Ourselves

It is now time for us to face the truth about ourselves. First, our trouble is internal. We tend to believe that something outside us causes temptation or neutralizes it. Not true. The trouble is on the inside. Unless we recognize our internal propensity to sin, and seek God's antidote, we have not really begun to deal with temptation.

Second, our trust must be in the eternal. Our only hope is found in the eternal One who has not a trace of evil in him, who changes not, who chooses to work in our lives, who offers us all that we need to remain steadfast. We can trust in him and draw on his strength. We can discover the resources he has given us to say no to evil.

Third, our behavior needs to follow the divine prescription. Like a doctor prescribing medicine for a physical ill, God also has written out a prescription for us. But unlike a physician's illegible scrawl, God's message is crystal-clear. Look at James 1:19-21: "Everyone should be quick to listen, slow to speak and slow to become angry, for man's anger does not bring about the righteous life that God desires. Therefore, get rid of all moral filth and the evil that is so prevalent and humbly accept the word planted in you, which can save you."

James addresses anger first, and for good reason. Many men don't know how to handle anger, often becoming loud or aggressive or even violent. While anger itself is not necessarily sin, when we give in to it and allow it to control us, it can become sin. God's prescription for anger is to be quick to listen, slow to speak, and slow to get angry. In those situations when you just want to make your point and win the argument, say to yourself, "This isn't going to achieve anything. This response to anger is inappropriate. It won't produce the life God wants."

A second area of concern is the "moral filth and the evil that is so prevalent." This certainly describes our world today as well as the first-century world. There are all sorts of things around us that are morally filthy. We can allow ourselves to feel comfortable with it, or even grow to like it. We can slosh around in all kinds of moral pollution and never notice the smell. Why? Because something inside us is attracted to filth. We need to be aware of that. And we need to get rid of it—which is easy to understand, but difficult to carry out.

For example, if you are in a relationship that you know is wrong or inappropriate, open your eyes to that fact. Then, once you're aware of it, take the next step and end it. Do you feel too weak to break off the relationship? Remember that our all-powerful God gives good and perfect gifts; he would never tell you to do something and not give you the resources to follow through.

Or perhaps your problem is pornography. Something inside of you responds to it and wants more, and now it is becoming addictive. You are hooked on it, and it is hurting your marriage or (if you are single) adversely affecting your relationships. What to do? Recognize that there is something morally filthy in your life, and admit that something in you is attracted to it. Then get rid of it. Cancel the subscription, avoid the newsstand, don't go down those aisles at the video store. Once we decide to take temptation seriously, taking action should not be too difficult.

The final part of the prescription for handling temptation comes in verse 21: "Humbly accept the word planted in you, which can save you." In other words, when you accept God's word as truth and begin to apply it in your life, you will discover the resources that can save you from everything that drags you down. As the Word of God takes root in you and begins to grow, you will respond differently to situations that arise. You will be more likely to view them as opportunities to do right. And when you feel the lure of temptation, you will have the God-given strength to resist.

That strength, combined with our desire to follow God's will and establish godly priorities, gives us the fortitude necessary to face temptation.

THE ROLES OF A
CHRISTIAN MAN

Go to the ant, you sluggard; consider its ways and be wise! It has no commander, no overseer or ruler, yet it stores its provisions in summer and gathers its food at harvest. How long will you lie there, you sluggard? When will you get up from your sleep? A little sleep, a little slumber, a little folding of the hands to rest—and poverty will come on you like a bandit and scarcity like an armed man.

Proverbs 6:6-11

6

Men Working

We spend approximately half of our waking hours working. That represents a major segment of our conscious lives. If you are like most men, you probably spend additional time thinking and talking about work even when you aren't on the job. Therefore, it seems important that we gain a good understanding of our attitude toward—and our relationship with—work.

There is certainly no shortage of wrong attitudes toward work. Most fall into one of three categories, or combinations of these: too casual, too involved, or too meaningless. People in the first group tend to see little significance in their work, and they show little interest in or enthusiasm for it. In response to this attitude, one business in New York City put the following notice on its employee bulletin board: "Sometime between starting and quitting time, without infringing on lunch periods, coffee breaks, rest periods, storytelling, ticket selling, holiday planning, and the rehashing of yesterday's television programs, we ask that each employee try to find some time for a work break. This may seem radical, but it might aid steady employment and ensure regular paychecks."

It seems to escape some people that the reason they go to

work is to work, not merely to socialize and then pick up a paycheck. Proverbs 6 has a few pungent words to say about such people, whom it terms "sluggards." In verses 6 to 8 we are told we can learn something about work by watching the ant: "Consider its ways and be wise! It has no commander, no overseer or ruler, yet it stores its provision in summer and gathers its food at harvest." Then, in verses 9 to 11, as well as in 26:13-16, we find a disparaging description of sluggards. They worship relaxation, are committed to procrastination and rationalization, and utterly lack motivation. In short, they have no sense of a biblical work ethic.

In the second category are people who go to the opposite extreme: They give so much time, energy, and attention to their work that it becomes an idol, and its products become gods in themselves. That is, some people work because they want the money, the status, and the symbols of prestige that work can bring. Their attitude is purely self-oriented. They neglect their family as well as their own spiritual growth, and they rarely perform voluntary service in their church or neighborhood. I came across an anonymous poem in the *Washington Post* that describes this all-too-common attitude:

Now I lay me down to sleep
I pray my Cuisinart to keep,
I pray my stocks are on the rise
And that my analyst is wise; . . .
If I go broke before I wake
I pray my Volvo they won't take.

A variation on this approach is the person who constantly

works or travels not primarily for the money but for a good organization or cause—even a Christian cause. Unfortunately, the resulting neglect of one's wife, children, church, and inner life may look no different than that of the money-grabbing opportunist.

The third kind of attitude occurs among people who feel a terrible sense of meaninglessness and aimlessness in their work. Their jobs often involve mundane, repetitive, assembly-line tasks that give little sense of creativity or accomplishment. In this kind of setting, it is easy for a "Thank God, it's Friday" attitude to develop, where everyone mindlessly puts in their time and watches the clock, waiting for quitting time, when their "real life" can begin.

Some time ago researcher Daniel Yankelovich conducted a survey of assembly line workers in the automotive industry. In a report of his findings entitled *New Rules*, he said, "Symptoms of worker frustration were visible everywhere . . . in absenteeism, tardiness, carelessness, indifference, high turnover, the number of union grievances, slowdowns in the periods preceding collective bargaining, and even sabotage. But mostly, worker frustration was seen in poor product quality." Further, twenty-seven percent of the workers in one particular factory indicated that under no circumstances would they buy the products they were making. If you find yourself in that kind of work situation, take a hard look at the career you are pursuing or the job you are doing.

A Biblical Work Ethic

Just what should be our attitude toward work? To find out,

let's go back to the very beginning of Scripture, to the creation of the world. At one stage in the creation process, "the Lord God had not sent rain on the earth and *there was no man to work the ground*, but streams came up from the earth and watered the whole surface of the ground" (Gen. 2:5-6, italics added). At a later stage, however, "The Lord God took the man and put him in the Garden of Eden *to work it and take care of it*" (Gen. 2:15, italics added). Clearly God's intention from the beginning was to put man to work. What's more, work also was something God engaged in himself. "By the seventh day God had finished the *work* he had been doing; so . . . he rested from all his *work*" (Gen. 2:2, italics added).

The creation order is perfectly straightforward—man is to work properly and rest adequately. There is a time to work and a time to rest. The Sabbath rest, which was to become a distinctive feature of the lifestyle of God's people, was introduced by God himself at the very start; when we ignore it, we pay the price physically, socially, and spiritually.

Two Important Characteristics of Work

From Genesis we also learn something about the nature of work: It is creative and it is productive. The work of God in creation and the work he assigned to Adam reflected each of these characteristics. So developing a proper attitude toward work means realizing we are manifesting the image of a creative and a productive God.

On my wife's desk stands a peculiar, homemade mug. It has a long nose, bulging eyes, and pale, swollen cheeks.

Made by one of our children in junior high, it has proved to be a great conversation piece. We often say to guests, "Which of our children do you think made this?" Without exception our friends look at it, laugh, and without hesitation say, "Pete, of course!" Dave is serious, Judy industrious, and Pete humorous. When you know that, you have no difficulty knowing who made the pottery, because the creation reflects the creator. So it is with people who know they are created; they long to reflect something of God's glory in the way they live and work.

They also feel a sense of wonder and purpose in everything they do. They cannot look dispassionately at either people or things, for everywhere they see something of the Creator's handiwork. No person is insignificant, and no part of the created order is without meaning. This sense of wonder makes created people worshipers—not only in the limited sense of attending church and singing praises, but also in the daily routine of life and work, where everything, no matter how mundane, is done with the sense that it is being done with God's materials, his time, and for his glory with the energy and skill he has given.

Enter Sin

All of this is part of the attitude God intended his people to have toward work. But when sin entered the world and Adam disobeyed God, the divine image he bore became seriously damaged. And so did the way he would interact with his work. Honest labor, for which he was created and which he knew God himself had delighted in, became toilsome and loathsome (Gen. 3:17-19).

Winston Churchill, standing in the wreckage of war-torn Europe, told the House of Commons on May 13, 1940, "I have nothing to offer but blood, toil, tears, and sweat"— words strangely applicable many centuries before to a man standing in the wreckage of a glorious garden. Life would become a struggle for survival, a battle against a physical world reluctant to yield its benefits. Discouragement and disillusionment would prevail, and man's wearisome struggle would end in futility, for his life would continue "until you return to the ground, since from it you were taken; for dust you are and to dust you will return" (Gen. 3:19). What man might have been and how he might have been transported from this scene we can only conjecture. What he became and what he heads toward is all too clear; simply visit a factory floor or a cemetery for proof.

Enter Meaning and Hope

Despite the effects of sin and the Fall, man still reflects something of the image of his Creator, even if the image is fuzzy or distorted. And Scripture continues to affirm the value of work as a form of service to God. Furthermore, many stories and teachings are scattered throughout the Bible about maintaining a proper attitude toward work.

Proverbs 6 makes it abundantly clear that industry—being productive and being creative—is a major part of the biblical work ethic. "Go to the ant, you sluggard" simply means to consider the activities of the ants and learn from their value system. Take even a cursory look at a colony of ants and you'll discover that they are as busy as bees. And it is not pointless activity. Their work is both creative and productive.

For example, study ants closely and you will notice that at various stages in their development they are suited for a particular task, sometimes for only one day. The next day they may have different abilities and an entirely different task. Even so, their system works beautifully. Ants know what they are doing, what they are capable of, what they are gifted for. They understand their objectives, and they work hard to accomplish them.

The New Testament has examples of its own. For thirty years, Jesus worked his way through life as a carpenter. Then he laid aside that occupation and committed himself to a specific ministry, at the end of which he prayed these very significant words: "I have finished the work you gave me to do." That work was the act of redemption, the act of rolling back the consequences of the Fall. If toil and tedium in work are a result of the Fall, those who come to know Christ see these characteristics redeemed. They begin to develop a new approach to work, viewing it as something they were created and redeemed for; they can dive into it with enthusiasm and delight. This is foundational to our understanding of work.

Six Ways to Approach Our Work

I have identified at least six scriptural principles that should inform our attitude toward work. As you move through this section, ask yourself, "How do these principles compare with my own work attitudes? Which attitudes are headed in the right direction? Which ones need to change, and how?"

Our ability to work is part of what makes us human. Yes, ants dig labyrinthine tunnels, bees make honey, spiders weave webs, and beavers construct dams. But human beings are uniquely creative and productive. When we compare what human beings have been able to do on this earth with that of animals, we're in a class of our own. That is because humans alone are created in the image of God. So the extent to which we engage in creative, productive activity determines the extent to which we are expressing something of our humanity. And the extent to which we don't demonstrates a deficiency in our understanding of what it means to be human.

In Genesis 1:26, God indicated that humankind should exercise dominion over his creation. Presumably this means that humans were given the creative ingenuity to move around in the divine creation, discover its wonders, and put them to use for the glory of God and the benefit of other humans. Think about it: Every moment of our lives we benefit from the ingenuity of other people. At the personal level, God has given us skills and abilities that we can use to make our own individual contribution to the world. As we discover and exercise these gifts to create and produce things for God's glory and the well-being of our global community, we further demonstrate our humanity.

Work is a means of service. Jesus made it clear that he had come into the world not to be served, but to serve. He had a keen appreciation of human need and was committed to meeting that need. He told his disciples to have the same attitude. For Christians today, that means a servant attitude in the workplace reflects the level of our discipleship. When a Christian works in an office or factory, there is at least one person with a desire to serve.

The way we work shows others what we believe. Jesus told his disciples that people who observed the way they lived would see their good works and glorify the Father in heaven. The same is true for believers in the workplace today. If you see people who are aimless and careless on the job, who regard their work as meaningless, they probably lack a theology of work and are not deriving their work ethic from God. But if you find workers who have a keen sense of purpose, who show a servant attitude, who apply themselves to their work, who are productive but do not grab for all the credit, they are demonstrating the kind of attitude all Christians should have. And they will be recognized and applauded.

God has called us to be coworkers with him. God made Adam his coworker in Eden by giving him tasks to carry out, such as tilling the soil and naming the animals. Throughout biblical history, God enlisted patriarchs, prophets, kings, and many others to carry out his will. In the New Testament, the apostle Paul specifically emphasized that we are coworkers together with God. Today, we may think that people in certain professions—such as ministry or missions or the helping professions—are working more closely with God to fulfill his purposes. But the truth is, if we are pursuing the work for which God has gifted us and which he wants us to be doing, we are just as much his coworkers as anyone else's.

I like the story of the pastor who visited with one of his parishioners who was a farmer. After walking around the farm, the two men sat on the veranda drinking coffee. The pastor, trying to be spiritual, said, "Isn't it wonderful to see what God has done in his creation?" The old farmer said, "It certainly is—but you should have seen what a mess it was when he had it on his own." Though humorous, the farmer's words were theologically correct. In one sense, God's creation on its own is raw, wild, untamed, untapped. But when man comes along as a divinely ordained co-worker (and, I might add, a responsible steward of the earth), it is amazing what can be accomplished. Crops can be grown to feed people. Energy can be produced to heat homes, provide electricity, and power vehicles and machinery. Medicines can be discovered to treat and prevent disease. There are thousands of other examples that exemplify how wonderful it is to be cooperating with God and his purposes in the work that you are doing.

Work is a form of worship. "Whatever you do," Paul wrote to the Colossians, "work at it with all your heart, as working for the Lord, not for men" (3:23). Some people work to please the boss. Some work only when the boss is watching. Some work simply to put in the time, or to pay for a lifestyle, or because they have to. Other people work because they believe that by exercising their abilities, channeling their energies, and using their time wisely, they are actually glorifying God. They did not create their skills, energy, or time; they are simply channeling those resources into creative, productive activity for the well-being of the community. This process in and of itself glorifies God— completely apart from the product or service that results. It is an act of worship.

I would suggest that an attitude of "work as worship" could totally revolutionize the workplace. It could happen if believers went to work on Monday morning not griping or merely discussing Sunday's football game, like everybody else, but applying themselves to their work as if it were an act of worship, as if they were producing for the Lord. Imagine what it would be like in your carpool if you said, "Good morning, here we go to worship." Or we would even do well to imitate Snow White's dwarfs, who sang as they went to work and whistled while they worked! But seriously, if we begin to think of work in terms of worship, our attitudes will be transformed.

When we work, we function as providers. The Bible has several insights to offer in this area. One is its assertion that if a man will not work, he should not eat (2 Thess. 3:10). That is about as straightforward as you can get. (But notice that the verse does not say, "If a man *can't* work he shouldn't eat" or, "If a man can't *find* work he shouldn't eat." Some people have been legalistically harsh on this point and have not attempted to understand the problems of the handicapped and the unemployed.) Those who have the ability and the opportunity to work—and don't—are failing to do what they were created to do.

I want to differentiate here, however, between work and employment. At present, many people are unemployed simply because there is no work available to them. Yet I believe that when there is no employment—that is, work for pay—available to us, we can still take advantage of opportunities for volunteer work. There are many possibilities in the community of believers or in a charitable organization to do something of significance. Such activity has intrinsic worth and dignity in God's eyes, even though there may be no payment.

Scripture also says that if we do not provide for those who are dependent on us, we are worse than unbelievers

(1Tim. 5:8). Work provides food, clothing, and shelter for our families. As a result, it is good in and of itself. But the benefits do not end with our own circle of family and loved ones. Paul, in his letter to the Ephesians, wrote, "He who has been stealing must steal no longer, but must work, doing something useful with his own hands, that he may have something to share with those in need" (4:28). In other words, we work not only to support our families, but also to give to people in need. To return to the scene of the carpool, consider what a joy it would be to greet coworkers by saying, "Here we go to work—just think of all the money we will be able to give away!" That is a biblical work ethic.

Another important reason we work and earn money is to support the work of the Lord. Helping to finance the meeting of spiritual needs is a natural extension of providing for the physical needs of our families and for others in need. What a privilege to be able to work in order to further the kingdom of God.

One final thought: God never intended that we work for only a certain number of years and then stop. If we reach a point where we can retire from the job at which we are employed, wonderful. But that does not mean we are to stop being creative and productive. We must never stop investing our life to the glory of God and channeling our energies for the benefit of the community. Instead, we continue to work for these ends in whatever ways we can.

When we no longer need to maintain civilization or meet human needs or spread the gospel, there will be no necessity for work. But I don't see that happening in the foreseeable future. As long as there are people on this earth, workers will be needed—especially men like you and me who can bring a truly biblical attitude to the workplace.

You may say to yourself, "My power and the strength of my hands have produced this wealth for me." But remember the Lord your God, for it is he who gives you the ability to produce wealth, and so confirms his covenant, which he swore to your forefathers, as it is today.

Deuteronomy 8:17-18

7

The Provider's Duty

I am now going to deal with an issue that is a subject of hot debate in some circles and a source of tension in many marriages: Should the husband be the sole provider or the primary breadwinner for the family? And what does it really mean for a man to be a provider?

Clearly, there is much to say about this topic, far more than can be covered in one chapter. So I will focus on four aspects of being the provider that you may not have considered before. Taken together, they add up to a full picture of the way we care for our family and the way we view our financial resources.

The Real Provider

Now for that nagging question, Should the husband be the sole provider? Absolutely not. On the surface, the most obvious reason is the harsh economic reality of living in the United States at the end of the twentieth century. Many families today simply cannot make ends meet on a single salary. If you are the sole income for your family and you are able to support them, I am happy for you. But that does not mean you or anyone else is *required* to be the only source of household income. I find nothing in Scripture to support this idea.

I believe there is an even deeper reason why the husband (or the wife, for that matter) should not be the lone provider. Consider the words God gave to the Israelites as they were about to enter the Promised Land: "You may say to yourself, 'My power and the strength of my hands have produced this wealth for me.' But remember the Lord your God, for it is he who gives you the ability to produce wealth, and so confirms his covenant, which he swore to your forefathers, as it is today" (Deut. 8:17-18).

A few years ago I came across an interesting quote in a book by Samuel Schultz, former professor of Old Testament at Wheaton College. He wrote, "A God-fearing person must always be conscious that all abilities are a divine endowment." If he is right—and I believe he is—then clearly we need to consider the whole area of wealth, finance, and provision as something flowing out from God-given ability. In that sense, none of us is a provider at all; God is the only true Provider. We are merely channels for managing and allocating God's provision.

Of course, we still have an important part to play. The Israelites were about to enter into the Promised Land—a good land, overflowing with springs and streams, wheat and barley, vines, fig trees, pomegranates, olives, and honey. There was iron in the rocks and copper in the hills. All of this had been divinely created and graciously presented to them. But the wheat would not thresh itself; the figs would not pick themselves; the olives would not press themselves; and the copper and iron would not dig themselves up. The Israelites needed to do the threshing, picking, pressing, and digging. They would contribute to the resources that God had provided.

At the same time, they needed to bear in mind that their prosperity and survival were the result of divinely created resources combined with their own divinely endued resourcefulness. God knew the children of Israel would be prone to forget this. So he told Moses to instruct them that when they got to the Promised Land and began enjoying all the things God had given them, they were to praise the Lord their God for his provision.

Here in the United States we have a special day, Thanksgiving Day, when we do just that. And many of us bow our heads and bless the Lord before we eat our meals. We do not bless the food—the food didn't do anything—we bless the Lord who has given it. It would be equally appropriate every time you walk through the door to bless the Lord for the roof over your head. And every time you draw your paycheck to bless the Lord for your paycheck. And every time you balance your checkbook or receive a dividend from your investments. Why? Because, directly or indirectly, all that you are and all that you have come from God.

That idea should give us a fresh context for thinking about who should be the sole or primary breadwinner in a family. The truth is, God is the real Provider. The burden of providing is on him, not us. Of course we have responsibilities to carry out—and we will address them shortly. But men must first realize that we are not required to live up to a standard that is nowhere mentioned in the Bible. Instead, we are to acknowledge God's divine provision, and then act responsibly in appropriating it.

Rights vs. Responsibilities

Nowadays every imaginable special interest group is

claiming it has the right to be officially recognized. Women and minority groups have been fighting for equal rights. Prisoners are demanding certain privileges while in jail. Families are declaring their right to be notified when convicted criminals move into their neighborhoods. There are right-to-life groups and right-to-die organizations. Many of these causes are good and necessary, but it seems our society is overly obsessed with standing up for its rights.

This has carried over into homes and families as well. Kids are demanding more from their parents, saying that they have the right to a car of their own or a free college education. Husbands and wives are appealing to their right to maintain a certain income level, to work or not work, or to work full-time or part-time.

Rights are important, but they need to be balanced by responsibilities. When it comes to providing for a household, every member of the family—not just the husband or just the couple—has rights and responsibilities.

The apostle Paul offers insight into striking a balance between the two. In 1 Corinthians 9:20-22 he explains how he reaches out to the lost: "To the Jews I became like a Jew, to win the Jews. To those under the law I became like one under the law . . . so as to win those under the law. To those not having the law I became like one not having the law. . . so as to win those not having the law. To the weak I became weak, to win the weak." Read the passage in context, and you will notice that Paul twice inserts parenthetical phrases to qualify what he has just said. I want to focus on the second such phrase, found in verse 21. Paul says, "I became like one not having the law (though I am not free from God's law but am under Christ's law)." In other words, he, as a believer in the gospel, recognized that

Christians come under the law of Christ.

When we come under the law of Christ, we live in a relationship with him. Part of that relationship involves recognizing our responsibility to Christ and our ultimate accountability to him. Our society does not place much emphasis on duty, responsibility, and accountability. Yet we have a sense of duty to the Lord Jesus that becomes a prime motivating factor in the way we live—and the way we care for and provide for our families.

An even more encompassing call to duty is found in Ecclesiastes 12:13: "Fear God and keep his commandments, for this is the whole duty of man." This defines a sense of responsibility even beyond that to king and country. It declares an allegiance or moral obligation to God himself. In light of this verse, the responsibility of providing for our families takes on a larger meaning. It is one part of our greater commitment and devotion to the Lord. If we are more concerned about individual rights and freedoms than our duty to the family and to the larger body of Christ, then we will have difficulty in the area of financial provision.

On the other hand, Paul does not suggest for a moment that rights are unimportant. To the contrary, he says that rights must be recognized. From the very beginning of 1 Corinthians 9, for example, he points out that he has certain rights because he is an apostle. One of those is the right to be recognized as one in whom specific authority resides and upon whom certain responsibilities rest (vv. 1-2). In verses 3-6, he points out his right to be respected as a human being: "Don't we have the right to food and drink? Don't we have the right to take a believing wife along with us, as do the other apostles and the Lord's brothers and Cephas? Or is it only I and Barnabas who must work for a living?" In verses 7-12, he uses many arguments to show that he has every right to be remunerated for his work as a minister.

When the apostle Paul talks about duty to the Lord Jesus, he is not suggesting that individual rights do not exist. Instead, he is saying that, while individual rights must be recognized, they must also be carefully regulated.

In addition, I believe Scripture teaches that rights are secondary to responsibilities. Carefully examine the Ten Commandments and you will discover little about human rights and much about human responsibilities. Take "Thou shalt not kill." God could have said, "You have the inalienable right to life." But he did not focus on the right. He focused on the responsibility. But interestingly enough, if people fulfill the responsibility, another person's rights are met. The only way that my right to life can be preserved and protected is by other people respecting me and accepting the responsibility not to kill me.

Not only are rights linked to responsibility, but Paul tells us in 1 Corinthians 9 that rights are always subject to restraint. Three times he speaks from his own experience: "We did not use this right" (verse 12); "I have not used any of these rights" (verse 15); "So [I do] not make use of my rights in preaching [the gospel]" (v. 18). "Yes, I've got my rights," he insists, "but all my rights are regulated by a prior commitment to my responsibilities."

Bringing this concept into a biblical balance is important because I feel there is an imbalance in our society. People tend to have a strong commitment to their individual rights—even within the family—without recognizing that these rights can only become true and real with a commitment to responsibility. The mature Christian accepts responsibility as primary and rights as secondary. He also recognizes that his primary reponsibility is to live under the law of Christ.

We are all born with a downward gravitational pull that biases us toward selfishness and sinfulness. That sin leads to death—spiritually, physically, eternally. The essence of the Christian gospel, however, is this: When you find yourself in Christ, the Spirit of the living God moves into your life, replacing the old law of sin and death with the new law of life in Christ. He counteracts the downward gravitational pull of sin and death, setting you free.

According to Paul, that freedom comes "in order that the righteous requirements of the law might be fully met in us, who do not live according to the sinful nature but according to the Spirit" (Rom. 8:4). You are set free, not to please yourself, but to fulfill the righteousness of the law. In other words, you are set free to live under the power of the Spirit, fulfilling a sense of duty, of responsibility, of accountability to the Lord Jesus, to whom you belong and whom you serve. That is why we can say today, "Because I belong to Christ, I have a responsibility to the people and the resources he has placed in my care—my family and my finances."

But perhaps that is a struggle. Do you find yourself more concerned about preserving and protecting your rights than about fulfilling your responsibilities? Do you find yourself motivated by a desire to honor the Lord Jesus Christ, under whose law you operate? Or are you constantly being pulled back into doing your own thing, pleasing yourself, going as you wish through life? I encourage you to realize that the Spirit of the living God has set you free from the old life in order that you might come under the law of Christ and sense your duty toward him and toward your family.

The Greed Factor

If people do have a sense of duty in our society, it is likely to be a sense of duty to themselves alone. Their driving concern is their own well-being, their own happiness, their own comfort and pleasure. Of course, if we have a society of people primarily interested in their own pleasure, and if the only duty they see is to themselves, it should be obvious that we have some major problems. The tragedy is that this attitude has infiltrated the Christian community—and Christian families— as well.

You may be saying, "That is certainly not me. I work long hours every week, sure, but I do it to provide for my family—so we can live in a nice neighborhood, my kids can have their own computers, and they can attend good private schools." Or maybe you are more like the person who says, "My own pleasure? That is the last thing on my mind. Both my wife and I are working full-time, but after you subtract our taxes, health insurance, and child care, we can barely cover the bills. So if we want to eat out now and then, and give the kids their Rollerblades and music lessons, we have to rack up our credit cards and stagger our bill payments. There is just no other way. I wish I had more money so I could be a better provider, but I'm doing all I can."

I would suggest that the motivation for both of these attitudes may be more related to greed than a desire for these men to provide for their families. Many of us are not aware of the powerful influence that material things exercise on our lives. We like to be comfortable, happy, and well cared for. But unless we are very careful, it is easy to become confused about the difference between a "need" and a "want." Before we know it, we end up consumed by our wants; this happens at both the individual and the family level. While we are busy providing for our wants—and our family's wants—we may be neglecting the needs of others. By focusing on our own wants, we may lose sight of the truly needy around us.

We should also be aware that because we live in a secularized world, we cannot help but be influenced by the secularism around us. The pressure of maintaining the status quo, the continual bombardment of materialistic advertising, and trendy philosophies all affect us. If these influences are not countered, they will make us more greedy and less sacrificial, more earthbound and less heaven-minded. We begin to believe that certain professions or income levels "require" us to live in exclusive areas or drive luxury cars or send our kids to prep schools. Even if we do not earn a lot of money, we may still be driven by the desire to pursue a higher standard of living, falling susceptible to the same kind of greed as those who are affluent.

However, as godly providers, we can counter these pressures.

First, continually expose yourself to the Word of God so that you might be aware of the real world of eternity, in touch with the real values of the eternal. When you find yourself lured by materialism, either at the personal or the family level, take steps to say no to yourself and yes to the Holy Spirit, yielding to what he has been saying to you through the Word of God, obeying him rather than your own desires, following his dictates rather than your own inclinations. This will require a considerable degree of personal insight, spiritual discernment, and disciplined behavior in the power of the Spirit of God. It will also require much dialogue and prayer among you and your other family members.

Second, inventory your own possessions and your budget. Take time to go back through your checkbook; review what proportion of your earnings went to yourself or for family pleasure, and how much was devoted to the concerns and needs of others. Evaluate the way you and your family spend your time and see how much of it is invested in yourself and how much is channeled into the work of the Lord. Look at your will and see how you have been approaching the future; what things are important enough to be remembered in the disposition of your estate?

Understand now that I am not telling anyone to cancel family vacations or to avoid making purchases that benefit their children or enhance family life. All of those things have their place. But what I am urging you to do is look at the bigger picture and strive for a balance between what you provide for yourself—individually and as a family— and what you give to others.

Then, once you have taken your inventory, sit down with the Lord and your budget. Say to him, "Lord, all I have is yours, including my family. As I attempt to allocate your provision in my life and in that of my family, keep me mindful of the end results of greed. Please show me how to budget my time, resources, and life so that all will be invested for you and eternity—not only for the sake of myself and my family, but also for needy people around the world."

Discipline in Providing

Finally, if God is the true Provider, and if my responsibility is first to him and then to my family, and if greed can so easily tip the scales toward our own priorities, it follows that we need to be conscientious stewards of all he has given us. As providers, we need to remember that our provision extends beyond ourselves and our families to the work of the Lord. Stewardship should be an integral part of that role.

There are two aspects of stewardship that we need to examine. The first is in Deuteronomy 8:5: "Know then in your heart that as a man disciplines his son, so the Lord your God disciplines you." God wanted his people to live orderly lives. He did not want their lifestyle to be excessive or unbalanced. In short, they needed discipline.

We all recognize this. If we do not exercise discipline in what we eat, our health will be jeopardized. If we do not exercise discipline in our sexual relations, we will do terrible damage to ourselves and to others. If we do not exercise discipline in our entertainment, we risk becoming addicted to the pursuit of pleasure. God wants his people to be disciplined in all dimensions of their lives. One of those dimensions is the handling of wealth that God has entrusted to us.

In Deuteronomy, God first tells his people that when they get into the Promised Land, they must discipline themselves to worship—that is, to praise the Lord for all he has given them. There were certain places, times, and procedures they must follow in order to learn the discipline of worship. According to Deuteronomy 12:6, after having told the Israelites where they were to worship, God says, "There bring your burnt offerings and sacrifices, your tithes and special gifts, what you have vowed to give and your freewill offerings." In another part of the Old Testament they were told by God, "No one is to appear before me emptyhanded" (Ex. 23:15). In another place in the

Bible they were told, "Ascribe to the Lord the glory due his name; bring an offering and come into his courts" (Ps. 96:8).

Part of the discipline of worship involved activities related to believers' resources. You may have noticed a little word hidden in that list of things—a word that strikes terror in the hearts of many people who sit in pews: the word *tithe*. The children of Israel were required by God to give to him ten percent off the top of all that they produced. "Wait," you may say, "are you suggesting we should do that today?" No, *I* am not *suggesting* that. God has *told* us to do it.

The final paragraph of Leviticus offers a straightforward picture of what we are to do: " 'A tithe of everything from the land, whether grain from the soil or fruit from the trees, belongs to the Lord; it is holy to the Lord. . . . Every tenth animal that passes under the shepherd's rod will be holy to the Lord' " (Lev. 27:30, 32). Ten percent of their harvest was to be brought to the place of worship and presented to the Lord to further his work.

In giving this command, God was building discipline into his people's lives. "It is absolutely imperative," he is saying, "that you not squander the resources I have entrusted to you." He holds the same desire for every one of us today. Not squandering God's resources means not spending a hundred percent of what you make on yourself or your family. It means that you look at your earnings in an orderly way, take ten percent off the top, and present it to the Lord. That is the principle of tithing. It builds discipline and it is obligatory.

I am very grateful for my dad's example in this area when I was a little boy. He ran a grocery store, and at the end of each day I would often stand and watch him count the proceeds from the day's business. As he would empty the till and count out the money, I noticed that he would put one tenth of it aside. The first time he did it I asked him why.

"Because one-tenth of this is not ours—it belongs to God," he explained. He had a special little box to keep it in, and whenever the need arose for something in the Lord's service, the resources were always there. Maybe you do not need two little boxes; maybe you need two bank accounts or two checkbooks. But we all need to recognize that tithing is a way to exercise discipline in our handling of God's resources.

One question I have been asked frequently about tithing is, "Should the tithe be based on your gross or net income—before taxes or after?" Here is a rule of thumb: If you have not gotten around to tithing the net—that is, your income remaining after taxes—then start by getting to that point. If you are already tithing your net income, then work your way up to tithing the gross. And once you are tithing the gross, then you are ready to start giving offerings above and beyond the tithe.

I realize this can be very difficult for those who were never taught to tithe. But as we move to adopt a thoroughly biblical approach to giving and providing, we can learn to adjust our lifestyle to how much we have left after giving to the Lord.

Devotion in Providing

God wants us to give a tithe of our income to him as part of providing for our family. The reason is that he wants us to build discipline in our management of his resources. But he not only wants us to exercise discipline; God also wants us to use our money to express devotion. The New Testament principle is captured in Matthew 6:21: "Where your treasure is, there your heart will be also." Your giving (that is, your special offerings) is a wonderful barometer of where your heart is.

Let me give an example. One day while the children of Israel were in the wilderness, God said to Moses, "Get the people to bring me a special offering—all those who are willing and all those whose hearts are stirred."

Moses asked, "What is it for?"

The Lord said, "Build me a sanctuary so that I may be present in the midst of my people."

And so the word went out from Moses: "God wants us to build a sanctuary so he may be present in our midst. To do it we will need all who are willing and all who are devoted to the Lord and his service to bring a special offering." This was not a tithe; the special offerings were optional.

The Israelites responded so overwhelmingly to God's request that the people in charge of building the tabernacle came to Moses and said, "Tell them not to bring anymore! We've got all that we can use." Moses commanded the people to stop their giving (see Ex. 35:4–36:7.) What a wonderful story! That is how it ought to be with the work of God.

Whatever ability you have to produce wealth is a gift from God. But regardless of the degree of our success, we have a responsibility to use our abilities and resources wisely, without greed, keeping the needs of others in mind. God has given each of us the opportunity to be disciplined and devoted stewards of our financial resources. As men grasp that truth—and faithfully live it out—we gain a fuller picture of what it means to be a provider.

Be imitators of God, therefore, as dearly loved
children and live a life of love, just as Christ
loved us and gave himself up for us as a fragrant
offering and sacrifice to God.

Ephesians 5:1

❖❖❖

8

What Do Real Husbands Do?

Paul Reiser, star of the TV sitcom "Mad About You," and his real-life wife, Paula, had a baby boy. Shortly afterward, a *USA Weekend* interviewer asked him, "Has your new baby changed you?"

"No," Reiser replied. "I change him."

Reiser and his TV character are certainly one of the "model husbands" that have floated through our consciousness. Another would be Tim Allen's bumbling but lovable character on "Home Improvement." Both represent the emergence of a "new" kind of husband and father, one who has shed the old Archie Bunker stereotype and has become an active participant in the marriage relationship and in the childrearing. Some men are even going so far as to take advantage of the Family and Medical Leave Act to take paternity leaves from work—coinciding with the maternity leaves of their wives—so they can stay home and care for their families.

These changes in our society seem to suggest that we are entering a more enlightened time, when "real men" accept the responsibilities of "real husbands." But what do real husbands really do? The biblical answer surfaces in Ephesians 5 and 1 Peter 3:7. From this base, we can examine three traits of a real husband.

Husbands Are Holy

Paul begins his teaching about husbands, wives, and children, slaveholders and slaves, by asserting that God's people are to be holy: "Be imitators of God, therefore, as dearly loved children and live a life of love, just as Christ loved us and gave himself up for us as a fragrant offering and sacrifice to God. But among you there must not be even a hint of sexual immorality, or of any kind of impurity, or of greed, because these are improper for God's holy people" (Eph. 5:1-3).

Distinctly Different Lives

The word *holy* makes many people uncomfortable, as if it meant absolutely perfect or sinless. But it simply means to be distinctive, to be different. God uses it to describe himself as well as his people. Christian husbands are to be different, distinct, and Scripture describes how that can be evidenced in at least three ways. First, we are to live a holy life in an attitude of love: "Be imitators of God, therefore, as dearly loved children and live a life of love, just as Christ loved us and gave himself up for us." For husbands, this is reinforced by verse 25: "Husbands, love your wives."

Why should this emphasis on love appeal to husbands and all believers? First, as Paul tells us, we are dearly loved children. As Christians we understand the love of God for us and have some insight into what love really means. This becomes the stimulus for a loving relationship in every area of our lives, particularly between husbands and wives. Real husbands can be holy because of their personal experience of the love of God.

Another factor prompting our love is that Christ loved us and gave himself up for us. The only reason we have peace with God is that our sins have been forgiven through Christ's love; without the love of God and Christ, we are nothing. Believers who recognize this begin to practice love. The Christian husband begins to love his wife in very specific ways. (For those unsure of how to love her, we will look later at the description of love in 1 Corinthians 13.)

Living in Light

The second way we are to be holy is to live in the light. "For you were once darkness, but now you are light in the Lord. Live as children of light" (Eph. 5:8). Living in darkness means to live out of touch with God, allowing evil and confusion to reign. But when we come to know Christ, we are introduced to the light and gain a new perspective on life.

Living in the light requires three separate actions. One, we must reject the darkness. Two, we need to reflect the fruit of light which Paul describes in verse 9: "The light consists in all goodness, righteousness and truth." When we live in the light of the knowledge of God through our Lord Jesus Christ, we become interested in what is good and right and true. That is a general rule for believers, but it is particularly true for a husband who wants to live a holy life in relation to his wife.

Three, we must respect the Lord's wishes as indicated in verse 10: "Find out what pleases the Lord." Then do it. Many men are only interested in pleasing themselves in marriage, and they expect their wives to assist them in that objective. Other husbands are only interested in pleasing their wives, and they do anything they can to keep them happy. Still others only want to please their peers and be "one of the boys," leaving their marital relationship to flounder. But a vital Christian relationship is based on something infinitely more important than pleasing yourself, your wife, or your peers. It is based on pleasing the Lord.

Living in the Lord

Finally, the third way to be holy is to live in the Lord. *The Living Bible* paraphrases verses 21 and 22 this way: "Honor Christ by submitting to each other. You wives must submit to your husbands' leadership in the same way you submit to the Lord." To live in the Lord, we must submit to him and to each other.

We gain the power to submit by allowing the Holy Spirit to work in us. Notice verse 18: "Do not get drunk on wine. . . . Instead, be filled with the Spirit." When we live in the fullness of the Spirit, a submissive attitude toward other Christians will naturally develop.

Marriages in the Greek world were disastrous for women. In her book *The Complete Woman,* Patricia Gundry explains that the "great men" of that day did not need wives for sexual fulfillment, love, or companionship. The temple prostitutes, who were superbly skillful in all kinds of erotic behavior, often satisfied men's sexual needs. In terms of love, many believed that true love could exist only between men, so homosexuality was rampant. Companionship was provided by female entertainers who were skilled in music, dialogue, and discussion.

So what role was left for the Greek wife? The Greek husband saw his wife as a fertile field. Just as a farmer sowed his seed in a fertile field to produce a crop, so did the Greek husband plant his seed in his wife to carry on the family. In other words, the Greek wife was a "baby machine." Because of this, it was customary for Greek girls as young as fourteen to marry men in their thirties.

The situation was little better among the Hebrews. Jewish wives also were regarded as fertile fields. In addition, they were not allowed to be in certain places, and their appearance was closely monitored: To appear in public with their hair hanging loose or uncovered was considered flagrantly seductive—and any wife so caught could expect an immediate divorce. In addition, Jewish women were regarded as morally and intellectually inferior to men and could not be witnesses in a court of law.

Strangely enough, similar inequities prevail today in Muslim courts. Some years ago when my wife and I were in Nigeria, we attended a trial with a friend. The entire courtroom suddenly rang with laughter at one point, and we were quite puzzled by it. Our friend explained that when a woman had stood to give her testimony, all the men in the room began to laugh. Then the judge himself started to laugh, banging his fist on his desk, doubling over with merriment. "What on earth is going on?" I asked. According to my friend, the judge had just reminded the woman that it takes the testimony of one hundred women to equal the testimony of one man. That is the way it is in Islamic Nigeria.

In addressing the inequitable situations of his own day, the apostle Paul said, "Come on, you Christians, show us that you are holy and distinctive. Make mutual submission the basis of a living, caring relationship in the power of the Holy Spirit. Establish marriages that are lived out in the light. Show this crazy world of ours what it is really like for a man and woman to live before the Lord in the fullness of his will for us."

We need to see holy marriages like this today.

The Husband As Head

Paul identifies the second function of a real husband in verses 23 and 24: "The husband is the head of the wife as Christ is the head of the church, his body, of which he is the Savior. Now as the church submits to Christ, so also wives should submit to their husbands in everything."

In contemporary usage, "head" means "boss." But is this a valid way of interpreting what Paul meant in this verse? We get some insight into his usage of "head" in Ephesians 4:15-16: "Speaking the truth in love, we will in all things grow up into him who is the Head, that is, Christ. From him the whole body, joined and held together by every supporting ligament, grows and builds itself up in love, as each part does its work."

These verses suggest that the head provides the whole body with sustenance for growing and building itself up in love. It is the source of life and blessing to the body. Also, the head is described as the integrating factor that joins the body together. In Ephesians 5, the head is variously referred to as the Savior of the body, the Lord of the church, and the lover of the bride. So if we are going to think in terms of headship (a word not found in the Bible), we must be careful not to simplify it to mean "the boss" or "the one in control." While the idea of authority is inherent in the word, "head" goes far beyond that basic concept.

For the man seeking to be a godly husband, headship involves servanthood. The husband's role is to be all that God wants him to be as provider for and encourager to his wife. His philosophy is "Not what I can get, but what I can give." He accepts the privilege of being a source of life and blessing to his wife. Instead of being authoritative and dictatorial, he is loving and caring. Frankly, if men fulfilled that role, I believe ninety percent of our society's marital problems would be solved.

The Husband As Heir

The third function of a real husband is identified in 1 Peter 3:7: "Husbands, in the same way be considerate as you live with your wives, and treat them with respect as the weaker partner and as heirs with you of the gracious gift of life."

This revolutionary teaching by Peter—that women were equally heirs of the grace of life—amazed the men of that time. For in Peter and Paul's day, men were the legal heirs of life. They strutted around and had everything going their way. Women entertained them, met their sexual needs, managed their homes, and produced sons (and heirs). Women were locked into roles determined by the men. But in Christ the husbands will see their wives differently and treat them accordingly—with deep respect and concern, not least because they are "the weaker partner." What Peter meant here, of course, has been the subject of considerable debate. However, women are certainly not morally or spiritually weaker than men, and given educational opportunities they have proved they are not intellectually weaker! Whether or not they are emotionally weaker will be a subject for discussion for years to come (but such discussion must include Margaret Thatcher, who regarded some men, particularly those on the other side of the aisle in Parliament, as "wimps"!).

Perhaps the clue to understanding Peter's point is to note that while his culture did regard women as morally and spiritually weak, that would be grounds for treating them with respectful concern rather than arrogant disdain. How much more important is it that we modern men who have a much more enlightened view of women should treat them properly?

Many of us men are extremely gifted at being inconsiderate. We fail to see the deep hurts and intense fears of our wives. We are notoriously insensitive—and the people we live with have the scars to prove it. It seems to be a characteristic of the male ego. Peter is telling us that because women are co-heirs with men of "the gracious gift of life," they are equally citizens of the kingdom of heaven.

So how do real husbands exemplify this attitude? They adhere to Jesus' teaching known as the golden rule: "Do unto others as you would have them do unto you." If husbands faithfully followed that precept in relating to their wives, the married women in our world would think they were on the threshold of heaven, if not halfway through the door!

Now Adonijah, whose mother was Haggith, put himself forward and said, "I will be king." . . . (His father had never interfered with him by asking, "Why do you behave as you do?").

1 Kings 1:5-6

9

Fathers and Their Children

The quality of fatherhood in Western society has declined steadily during this century, due in part to the Industrial Revolution, which took fathers away from home and into factories. But the shift also reflects a variety of secular trends and values that have led many men away from a biblical approach to fathering. To become fathers of honor and integrity, it is essential that we understand the biblical view—considering both how not to father (using the negative example of David and his children) and how to father well (looking at the positive example of God the Father).

I personally know many fathers who are struggling with their kids. They ask, "Where did I go wrong?" and deal with a tremendous load of guilt. In some instances, of course, mistakes have been made that need to be confronted and resolved. But in other cases fathers have done what they understood to be right, endeavoring to live as faithful examples, yet children have not turned out the way they would have hoped—or the way the Lord desires. This gives all fathers a great deal of concern. So in these pages I want to be honest and straightforward about scriptural teaching, while being sensitive to the real struggles many fathers are experiencing with their children.

First we will look at the way David behaved toward his children, as well as the way they turned out. Then, in marked contrast, we will look at the way God the Father treats his children, with particular reference to the way he responded to David as his child. Finally, we will apply some of the lessons we have learned to our own parenting experience.

A Great King, a Flawed Father

Three sons of David are mentioned in the Scripture passages we will examine: Amnon, Absalom, and Adonijah. We will look at them in that order, which happens to be from oldest to youngest.

Amnon

In 2 Samuel 13 we read that one of Amnon's friends noticed he had lost his appetite and thought he recognized the symptoms of love. So he went and asked Amnon, "Are you in love?" Amnon admitted that he was.

"Well, are you going to tell me who the girl is?" his friend inquired. "You can tell me; I'm your friend."

"All right. It is my half sister."

"What?!"

"That's right—my half sister," Amnon said. "My father, David, has all these different wives and concubines. Tamar is my half sister by one of those wives, and she is the most beautiful girl in Jerusalem. I'm hopelessly in love with her and I don't know what to do."

So Amnon's friend said, "Pretend to be sick. Knowing your dad, he will drop everything and come to see you. When he visits, tell him that your half sister Tamar is a magnificent cook and what you really need is some of her cooking. He'll send her over to your house. Then you've got her!"

The plan worked exactly as expected, and when Tamar came over to cook supper for her half brother, he raped her. Worse, the tremendous "love" that he had had for her instantly turned to hate and revulsion. He threw her out of the house and allowed it to appear as if she had precipitated the whole action. She suffered the abuse of being raped, as well as the ostracism of the community.

When David learned what had happened, he was furious. But that was as far as his reaction went. He did not do anything about it. The boy he raised had raped his own daughter, and the best he could come up with was being furious.

Absalom, on the other hand, was Tamar's full brother—and a very protective brother at that. When he heard what Amnon had done to his sister he wanted revenge, but he decided to wait until the time was right. For two years he held onto his cold, suppressed fury and plotted against his brother. Eventually he had Amnon murdered. And David's reaction to the murder of his son? He mourned deeply for him.

Absalom

Absalom prided himself on his very long hair, caring for it in every way imaginable. In fact, he did something that even men today probably have not thought of doing with their hair: Every time he had it cut, he weighed it.

For two years after Amnon had raped Absalom's sister Tamar, Absalom awaited his opportunity for vengeance. At last he carefully set the stage for revenge at the annual sheep-shearing festivities. First, he invited his father David to come, but the king declined—just the answer Absalom wanted. Then he said, "All right, could you send my brother Amnon down in your place?"

Knowing about the tenuous relationship between the two brothers, David was suspicious. "Why do you want him down there?" he asked.

"I just want him there to represent you, that's all."

"Well, okay," David said, ignoring his instincts. Sure enough, when Amnon arrived for the party, Absalom ordered his men to get him drunk and kill him.

Scripture contains no mention of any confrontation between Absalom and David, nor of any serious punishment issued for Absalom's deed. He did go into exile for three years, but by using Joab, David's righthand man, and a skillful means of deception, Absalom returned to Jerusalem. David, however, would not make an effort to see him for two more years.

Two years was too long for Absalom, who said, "I'm missing my father—I want to see him." He sent for Joab and told him, "Arrange for me to have an audience with the king." But Joab did not want to get caught in the middle. Yet Absalom would not accept no as an answer. So he ordered his servants to set fire to one of Joab's barley fields, thinking, "That will get his attention." It did. Even Joab was intimidated by Absalom, who demanded a second time that Joab arrange for him to see his father. This time he even went so far as to declare, "If I have done anything wrong, let my father put me to death!" Imagine a man who murders his brother, refuses to acknowledge any wrongdoing, and then challenges his father to face him. He had become totally convinced that whatever he did was right and that he could get away with it.

This time Joab promptly did what he was told and arranged for a meeting between Absalom and David. *Well,* you might think, *maybe David will really stick it to Absalom now.* Not this time. When Absalom came in, David hugged and kissed him. No confrontation. No honesty. No discipline.

After that, Absalom went further. He decided that he was going to become king in his father's place. He began getting up early in the morning and going to the factory gates while the guys were coming in and saying, "Hi, I'm Absalom. I'm running for king." His campaign worked. Scripture notes that Absalom "stole the hearts" of the people. And having done so, he was able to organize an uprising that actually overthrew the rule of King David. The Bible gives us a pathetic picture of David as he retreated up the Mount of Olives—barefoot, in tears, his clothes torn—lamenting the fact that he would be going into exile because his own son had ousted him.

With David gone, Absalom decided that he wanted to show everybody who was boss. He asked his advisor, Ahithophel, for suggestions. Ahithophel said, "Your father left ten of his concubines to look after the palace while he is in exile. We will set up a pavilion for you on the palace rooftop, and you can go up there and have sex with all ten of them in full view of Jerusalem. They will see what kind of a man you are, that you are afraid of neither man nor beast—not even your father the king—and they will give you their allegiance." So Absalom did just that, much to everyone's horror.

In the end, Absalom even challenged David and his army in battle. But as he was riding his donkey through the forest, his huge head of hair got caught in an oak tree. The donkey kept going and left him dangling there, helpless. Joab took advantage of the opportunity and put three spears through Absalom's heart. When David heard the news of his son's death, he cried out, "O my son Absalom! My son, my son, Absalom! If only I had died instead of you—O Absalom, my son, my son!"

Do you see a pattern developing in David's handling of both Amnon and Absolom? If you are still not sure, you will definitely see it in his treatment of son number three, Adonijah.

Adonijah

In 1 Kings 1:1-6 we find an old and decrepit King David lying in bed, unable to stay warm even when covered with blankets. But his young son Adonijah sat beside him, rubbing his hands and saying, "Now is my chance to be king." And so another son, never having learned from the experience of his brother Absalom, usurped the throne of his father David.

Notice a very interesting parenthetical statement in 1 Kings 1:6: "His father had never interfered with him by asking, 'Why do you behave as you do?'" I do not think this sentence should be in parentheses—it should be underlined in red!

The pattern is clear. Scripture is pointing out a marked link between the way David behaved toward his children and the way they behaved toward him. Of course, discipline and punishment of children can be taken too far. That does not mean it should be avoided altogether.

David and His Children

In characterizing David's behavior toward his children, Scripture first highlights the fact that there was an abundance of affection. When the newborn infant of his adulterous tryst with Bathsheba became ill, David prostrated himself on the ground for an entire week, refused to wash himself, refused to eat, and was mortified at the thought that this tiny, helpless baby was going to die. When Amnon, who perpetrated this terrible rape of his sister, was murdered, David mourned. When Absalom went off into exile after the murder, David longed to go to him, day and night. Finally, when Absalom was killed, David mourned uncontrollably. There is absolutely no question that David loved his kids to distraction. Having affection for your kids is good, but having too much affection, especially when their behavior dictates otherwise, can be quite harmful.

Second, the Bible suggests that there was a total breakdown of example on David's part. In fact, God had told David categorically that the very things he had done would not only be reproduced in his sons because of his example, but they would be magnified (2 Sam. 12:7-12). "David," he said, "you took another man's wife in secret; someone close to you will take your wives in public. You engaged in subterfuge, deceit, and manipulation; I will make sure that you experience an even greater degree of deceit and manipulation. Like father, like son."

A number of years ago I visited a longstanding friend of mine from Jamaica, Harland Hastings, who now lives in Halifax, Nova Scotia. We had not seen each other in some time, and we naturally talked about our kids.

"So what's Steve doing?" I said.

"Well," he replied, "Steve's in seminary. His main interest is in reaching West Indians in England. He is deeply concerned for them. He has a real missionary heart."

"And Pete?"

"Pete's in med school. He is a great student with a keen mind. Plus he has tremendous compassion for people."

"What's Harland Jr. doing?"

"Well, he is one of the top swimmers in Canada. He's the star of the Canadian water polo team and is currently training for the Olympics. Oh yeah, I forgot—Pete also coaches the water polo team for Nova Scotia."

Pretty impressive, but I wasn't the least bit surprised. Why? Because Harland Hastings is a brilliant physician who, as a student in Britain, advanced so quickly in his medical studies that he did surgery in his spare time. He is a fellow of the American College of Surgeons, the Royal College of Surgeons, and the Royal College of Physicians. In addition to his medical achievements, he found time to become the boxing champion and swimming champion of Scotland, and later he coached the Scottish water polo teams. Not to mention that he has also done missionary service and has a wonderful way with people.

Of course, no father can force his kids to turn out a certain way. But there is probably no stronger human factor in the way our kids turn out than the kind of example we give them. They are going to see some things they love, some things they like, and some things they never want to be. But dads, we should never underestimate the power of our example, good or bad. David, unfortunately, did not recognize this.

Third, there was a lamentable absence of discipline. One of David's fatal flaws in raising his kids was that he never interfered with or even questioned their behavior (1 Kings 1:6). At the very times when they should have been learning discipline from a self-controlled father, discipline never came. As kids they never had it. As men they didn't want it.

Fourth, David's children were spoiled. Whatever they wanted, they could have. Look again at the account of Amnon and Tamar in 2 Samuel 13. Tamar had prepared a meal for her brother, who then said he wanted to sleep with her. She said, "No, don't do this terrible thing." He said, "I don't care how terrible it is, I want you."

Then Tamar told her brother, "Look, just talk to David about it and he will arrange for me to be given to you in marriage." She knew that such a relationship was forbidden by law, but she also knew that Dad could get around any law for his kids. He would do anything for them. In other words, he spoiled his kids rotten.

Fifth, there was a terrible lack of guidance as far as David's children were concerned. They did not seem to grasp even elementary things. Take for instance Deuteronomy 5:16, which says, "Honor your father and your mother, as the Lord your God has commanded you, so that you may live long and that it may go well with you in the land the Lord your God is giving you." Fathers, your children under God are to be brought up to honor and respect their parents. And they learn to do it from people who start teaching them from the earliest days. If they grow up not to respect their parents, the reason is probably a breakdown in the way this principle has been articulated and modeled. Certainly this was true for David.

Here is another teaching David's children did not grasp: "If a man has a stubborn and rebellious son who does not obey his father and mother and will not listen to them when they discipline him, his father and mother shall take hold of him and bring him to the elders at the gate of his town. They shall say to the elders, 'This son of ours is stubborn and rebellious. He will not obey us. He is a profligate and a drunkard.' Then all the men of his town shall stone him to death. You must purge the evil from among you. All Israel will hear of it and be afraid" (Deut. 21:18-21).

Now, I am not advocating today that we stone our rebellious children, but this passage certainly demonstrates that in those days rebellious kids were taken seriously and full responsibility for them fell on the parents. Parents must make sure their kids grow up knowing to respect them. But ultimately we cannot mandate how our kids turn out. They have wills of their own, and they are responsible agents themselves. But in Old Testament times, if children did not grow up to honor their parents, the parents had the authority to take them before the ruling elders and actually have them put to death.

This is how David was supposed to have administered the law in his day. But he failed to do it. He was so wrapped up in his kids—wanting them to be happy, wanting them to have anything they asked for—that he never questioned them, never rebuked them, never challenged them, never disciplined them, never taught them. He allowed them to grow up wild. And he lived to regret it.

God and His Children

In contrast to the way David handled his children, let us look at the way God fathers *his* children, specifically in the way God handles David himself. It is a fair comparison, I believe, because in Ephesians 3:15 Paul refers to God the Father, "from whom his whole family in heaven and on earth derives its name." Literally, that passage means, "the Father, after whom all fatherhoods are named." In other words, if we want to get a handle on earthly fatherhood, we must look at the Father in heaven.

The first thing we learn about our heavenly Father is that he loves his children. Although we probably all know this, it cannot hurt to be reminded. Human beings were created in God's image, and even David's name, which means "beloved," reflects the bond between God and people. God loves his children.

But we also know that God loves his children enough to rebuke them when they misbehave. Look at what he did to David. When David committed adultery with Bathsheba, then arranged for her husband to die in battle, God sent Nathan the prophet to outline in public the horrendous things David had done. God never feels that his love for us means he should not correct us. In fact, it is precisely because God loves us that he insists on rebuking us in our sin. But we are rebuked so that God might bring us to repentance, which leads to his forgiveness. This was Nathan's intent when he came to David; he began his pronouncement by stating that the Lord had forgiven the king. Why? Because the Lord loved David, had rebuked David, and because David had responded to the rebuke by admitting his sin.

But look closely at what happened next. Once God told David that he was forgiven, he also said that he was going to be punished. And sure enough, in a remarkable way God began to carry out the punishment. This is how God deals with his children: He loves them, rebukes them, forgives them, and punishes them.

There are several reasons God punishes us. He does it first to preserve his own integrity. David's problem was that he was a soft touch, and his kids knew it. They knew that this fearsome King David, the man who slew the giant Goliath, was putty in their hands. They knew that this man who could organize the biggest empire they had ever seen could not run his own family. And because his sons got this passive picture of earthly fatherhood, they probably thought God the Father was like that too.

But God says no. "You will live with the consequences of all your actions and I personally will see that you do. I will bring punishment upon you. If I do not, I will be misunderstood and disregarded. I am not like your father David. I am holy."

God also punishes his children because he wants to confound his enemies. If David had gotten away with his sin, his enemies could have said, "See? All this stuff about God being God is nonsense. And all this talk about righteousness and accountability—it too is a lot of nonsense."

But God does not allow them that chance. He says, "David will live with the consequences of what he has done, because I don't want anybody to get the idea that the heavenly Father allows his enemies to blaspheme his name or question his integrity."

The third reason that God punishes his children is so that they might mature. In Hebrews 12:6-7 it says, "The Lord disciplines those he loves, and he punishes everyone he accepts as a son." Why? In order that they might reap a "harvest of righteousness and peace" (12:11). That means we are only going to mature as Christians when we fully recognize that God means business. This is one of the great tragedies in our world today—people think God is soft and easy. Pull his string and he will dance for you; ignore him and get away with it. In truth, God will take steps to insure that people do not get that idea.

Finally, God the Father encourages his children. Consider the aftermath of David's sin with Bathsheba. After their infant child died, David went to the grief-stricken mother, terribly conscious that they had not only lost a child, but that they had sinned before the Holy One of Israel. Humbled and heartbroken, he comforted her, and she conceived and bore a second son, Solomon, whose name means "loved of God." That son became Israel's second-greatest king and is listed in Matthew 1 as one of the ancestors in the lineage of Jesus Christ. That is just like God: always eager to give us a second chance, to encourage us to keep moving forward with our lives.

Today's Dads and Their Children

What a stark contrast between the fatherhood of David and the fatherhood of God. But what about our own fatherhood? How should we raise our children in today's world?

The Fear of the Lord

First, we must promote the fear of the Lord. I have given King David quite a beating in this chapter—or, rather,

Scripture has. But there is a beautiful passage that his son Solomon wrote years later:

Listen, my sons, to a father's instruction; pay attention and gain understanding. I give you sound learning, so do not forsake my teaching. When I was a boy in my father's house, still tender, and an only child of my mother, he taught me and said, "Lay hold of my words with all your heart; keep my commands and you will live. Get wisdom, get understanding; do not forget my words or swerve from them." (Proverbs 4:1-5)

After the sad story of David's dealings with his older boys, young Solomon came along. David, according to Solomon's own testimony, spent time with him, teaching him and encouraging him in the fear of the Lord.

Perhaps you are wondering how David could be such a pious example for Solomon after all the evil he had done. It is because he did not hide from his sin. He was honest about his shortcomings and mistakes. For example, when David wrote Psalm 51, that great penitential song, he immediately sent it off to the chief musicians, instructing them to set it to music. "I want the choir to sing it on the Sabbath," he told them. "I want everybody to know that I have written it and that it is my own personal expression. There is nothing hidden about my penitence, my repentance, or my confession."

As young Solomon heard about and no doubt witnessed other events like this one, he grew up knowing his father was not pretending to be perfect. He knew that when his dad blew it, he then set the record straight. But David did not just admit he was not perfect. He went further. He said to Solomon, "This is what I am and this is what I have done, Son. But the reason I want to set things straight is because I fear the holy righteousness of our God."

Are we instilling such an understanding and respect for God in our children today?

An Example of Godliness

Second, we must provide a godly example—but it has got to be an example that resonates with kids. Our generation is not interested in the same things kids are interested in. If you want them to get excited about being godly, let them see godliness in terms that are exciting and thrilling and winsome and attractive to them.

Our task as fathers is to build the kind of relationship with our kids that allows us to invest in them and learn how they think and feel. But it also should allow them to get to know who we really are and to see our godly example shining through.

A Relationship of Love

We must protect the relationship of love at all costs—that is, rugged love, tough love, whatever you want to call it. It is not David's soft, sentimental, anything-goes, don't-upset-them, don't-question-them, don't-interfere-with-them, don't-discipline-them, lavish-everything-upon-them love. That is not real love. True parental love is desperately concerned for our children's total well-being. It is careful to rebuke, correct, and instruct in righteousness so that our kids truly will grow up.

Honesty about Evil

Finally, we must warn them when evil pops up in their lives. We need to be involved in their lives enough to see it, identify it, make our protests about it, and let them know exactly where we stand on it. If we fail, we may end up producing exactly what we don't want to produce in our children.

Having and raising children is one of life's most awesome mysteries. It is incredible to think that we can be physically responsible for bringing into the world an entity of eternal significance made in the image of God—and that having done it, as fathers we are then responsible under God for the nurture and training of that human being. We need to pray every day that our sons and daughters might be brought up in the fear and admonition of the Lord, be responsible members of society, adhere to biblical principles, and ultimately come to know Jesus Christ personally.

May we all learn from the fathering mistakes made by David. And may we look always and often to the example of our heavenly Father, after whom all fatherhoods in heaven and earth are named.

A man of many companions may come to ruin,
but there is a friend who sticks closer than
a brother.

Proverbs 18:24

10

The Cost of Friendship

In *The Seasons of a Man's Life*, Daniel Levinson writes, "Friendship is largely noticeable by its absence. Close friendship with a man or woman is rarely experienced by American men." Those who are concerned about our society—and the emotional and spiritual state of today's men—recognize that we are often impoverished because of the superficiality of our relationships. Even among Christians, deep friendships between men, or close, platonic friendships between men and women, are quite scarce.

Scripture makes it clear that our lives are lived in terms of relationships—with God and with human beings. These relationships operate at many different levels, but in this chapter we will try to answer the question, "Are real friends necessities or luxuries for a man?" Friendship is a crucial aspect of our lives, and the Bible has much to say about it.

The Divine Dimension

Although most of us probably do not often reflect on it, the Christian's best friend of all is God himself. I cannot imagine a more exciting opportunity.

The Bible frequently talks about people who were "friends" of God. The book of Exodus tells us that God would "speak to Moses face to face, as a man speaks with his friend" (33:11). Abraham was called "the friend of God." But the statement that we can perhaps relate to more than these was spoken by Jesus in John 15. He reminds his disciples that he is their master, their Lord, their Savior, and that they are his servants. But then he says, "I am not going to talk to you as if you are my servants; I am going to talk to you as my friends." He shows them that he has opened his heart to them.

The Scriptures point out to us, however, that if we are to be the friends of God—and if we are to regard Jesus as a particular and special friend—we need to bear something in mind. In the words of the apostle James, remember that "friendship with the world is hatred toward God" (4:4). We cannot regard God and his son Jesus as our friends if we are committed to a secular attitude toward life.

Take a moment for a personal inventory of your relationship with God. Do you relate to God as your friend, feeling that you have heart-to-heart communication with him? Are you completely honest and transparent with him? We can go further: Do you relate to the Lord Jesus as your friend? Can you honestly say that you regard him as your intimate friend?

This is the level at which we ought to be able to identify our spiritual relationship.

The Human Dimension

Richard Fowler, in an article in *Discipleship Journal,* points out that friendships operate at five different levels.

The generality level. This is the stage of first encounter, when we bump up against somebody whom we have never seen. We may respond by saying to ourselves, "Hmm, I'd like to get to know him (or her) better." It is equally possible that our reaction is, "Yuck! Get me out of here."

Fowler says that, according to scientific observation, thirty percent of the people we meet in these first encounters dislike us immediately. We do not have to say a word; they are just turned off. Recognizing this, we should find encouragement in knowing that seventy percent evidently think we are not so bad. And actually we can tell ourselves to relax as far as both groups are concerned; there's the possibility of getting to know them at a different level.

The accommodating level. This level is not as superficial as bumping elbows, but it does not move much beyond being an arm's-length relationship. For whatever reasons, we find ourselves with these people. Although we want to get along with them—something about them is attractive and interesting—we have no initial intention of developing any degree of intimate relationship with them.

This can be seen often in a church congregation. The problem with this arm's-length relationship is that there is a minimum of reality in it. We are still operating at a level high in superficiality, play-acting, posturing, projecting. At the accommodating level, we deal basically with perceptions; we do not really know the person and he or she doesn't know us. We just sort of get along.

The teamwork level. This level develops once you and someone with whom you may have been "bumping elbows" find a common objective. You discover that now you are not just at arm's length; you are putting your shoulders to a common task. As a result you experience a certain camaraderie. And when you do, the relationship becomes more realistic.

Some years ago our church people recognized how large our congregation was growing, so we created small groups and encouraged people to get into them in order to be nurtured and mutually cared for. As a result, people joined in a common task and came to know each other as they never had before. For two years most of the groups met regularly, with good results. Then something happened that most of these people had not expected. As they got past the stage of superficial pretense, some acknowledged that they disliked others in the group. "We would rather have nothing to do with one another," they told me. At that point they began to level with each other and minister to each other—and the possibility existed of moving into the fourth level of friendship.

The "significant other" level. Out of their group, some began to discover a certain compatibility and commonality. They opened up more and more to each other—to such an extent that they got past the like/dislike stage. They trusted their newfound friend. They could be vulnerable with the other person, knowing that he or she would probably be vulnerable in return. In this way, they discovered something mutually beneficial in the relationship.

Most people will have this kind of relationship with no more than ten or fifteen people in a lifetime. But when you do, you can move beyond that stage into the fifth level.

The intimate level. At this level, which you might expect to experience with one or two people, you have such intimacy that just about anything goes in terms of concern and support and nurture for one another.

The Bible, as I have said, has a lot to say on the subject

of friendship, and it suggests quite forcibly that we ought to be cooperating on all of these five levels if we are to properly grow in community with one another. The next step is to look more closely at the relationships in which we can expect to experience friendships at these levels.

Male-Female Relationships

If you are married, it is hoped that your wife is your very best friend. You two are long past the bumping-elbows, arm's-length, and common-objective stages. You have seen things about each other that are mutually attractive and mutually beneficial, and you have come to the point of commitment and transparency. As intimate friends you are constantly nurturing and encouraging each other.

This is suggested powerfully in Proverbs 2:16-17. Speaking about an adulteress, the writer says she is a "wayward wife with her seductive words, who has left the partner of her youth and ignored the covenant she made before God." The word translated "partner" is translated in other passages as "close friend," suggesting that the person to whom you are married should be your partner, your close friend, the one with whom you have intimacy. One of the most enriching things that can happen to a man is to have a marital relationship that is based, among other things, on a very intimate friendship, one in which you thoroughly enjoy each other.

Yet marriage is not the only arena in which a man and a woman can have a healthy relationship. That does not mean, though, that such relationships are easy. I was talking to a group of young, single women from our church, and they told me that one of their problems is that they would like very much to make friends with young men on a nonromantic, nonsexual basis. They told me they would like to learn how to relate to Christian young men and to experience the mutual encouragement of such a relationship, but it is awkward and difficult. It is possibly even more awkward and difficult for married men to develop helpful relationships with other women, because they can easily go wrong.

However, if we cannot have nonromantic, nonsexual relationships with people of the opposite sex, we are impoverished. The church of Jesus Christ gives us a magnificent opportunity for developing these healthy, helpful relationships. The Lord Jesus himself illustrated this. On numerous occasions in the Gospels we read of the close friendships he had with women. And this was something that was even more unusual in his day.

Same-Sex Friendships

Anyone who has observed the female scene will recognize that women appear to make friends easier than men do. They seem to be more open to developing relationships. Some time ago, my wife, Jill, wrote a book entitled *Thank You for Being a Friend*. While she was writing that book I was helping her refresh her memory about certain relationships she had had over the years, and it was intriguing to me how many different, rich relationships Jill has enjoyed. I remember thinking that men do not often experience friendship that way.

So what about friendships between men? Levinson writes, "Most men do not have an intimate male friend of the kind they recall fondly from boyhood." It is a sad commentary on our society that now a man who has a close relationship with another man is suspected of homosexuality. But that is more a reflection of our perverted society than it is a statement on the validity of close, male relationships. Perhaps we men are not open to this kind of thing because we recognize that it requires time and sacrifice, transparency and honesty. Maybe we are not prepared to accept the vulnerability that goes along with those qualities. As a result, men often know nothing of relationships such as those between David and Jonathan, Peter and John, Paul and Barnabas, and Abraham and Lot.

The Friendship of Youth and Mature Age

One of the lovely illustrations in the New Testament of friendship between an older person and a younger one is the relationship between Barnabas and John Mark. Barnabas was the older colleague of the apostle Paul, and John Mark was the young fellow who left them during their first missionary journey. He blew it. When Paul said he wanted nothing more to do with John Mark, Barnabas stuck up for him. He chose John Mark to accompany him, their friendship was nurtured, and they continued working together.

I look back with tremendous gratitude to a man who came into my life when I was a young teenager during the Second World War. He was at least thirty years older than I. I was beginning to question Christianity, particularly the brand I had been introduced to as a boy. I did not question the faith of my father and mother; I knew their belief was genuine, and I embraced it heartily. It was just that their particular *expression* of it seemed dull to me.

But one morning this man marched into our little church, resplendent in the uniform of the Royal Artillery. He was a captain, a heroic man, and he became my friend. He went out of his way to befriend me, establishing a relationship that lasted until his recent death. Even when he was in his eighties, he still wrote to me and told me exactly what I needed to hear, whether I wanted to hear it or not. He did not change at all in his commitment to me and interest in me. For forty years I knew this relationship, and I was extremely grateful for it.

The Friendship of Youth and Youth

We know that young people frequently experience negative peer pressure. If they identify with other youths who have an unhealthy influence over them, there is an increased likelihood they will go wrong; in adolescence, what their friends think is more important to them that what their parents say.

But peer pressure is not all bad. Being such a powerful influence, it can actually help if it reinforces positive behavior. That is why it is so important that young people develop the right friendships—and that parents commit themselves to nurturing those friendships along.

Parents who want their kids to grow up to be healthy, mature Christians make the effort to ensure that their children are surrounded by healthy, growing young Christians. We shouldn't expect our youth to develop a mature Christian lifestyle if they spend most of their time with unbelieving kids—if we let them run wild because we cannot be bothered or because we are more interested in their playing ball than getting into a youth group. To grow up well, they need positive peer pressure.

The Prize of Friendship

"So what's in it for me?" That is the question, of course, that immediately comes to mind when we consider the sacrifices that go with friendship. If I am going to give of myself, be vulnerable, be open—if I'm going to nurture people, work with them, and spend time with them—what benefits will I get out of it?

The Longing to Belong

First, friendships give us the opportunity to meet our need to belong. No one wants to be regarded as irrelevant or insignificant. No one wants to think, "If something happened to me today, nobody would miss me." We would feel devastated if we believed we could disappear off the face of the earth without anyone even noticing.

According to Scripture, this need for belonging can be wonderfully met through friendships. Proverbs 17:17 says, "A friend loves at all times, and a brother is born for adversity." Having somebody who will always love you and be with you through difficult times—this is part of the prize that is friendship. Proverbs 18:24 adds, "A man of many companions may come to ruin, but there is a friend who sticks closer than a brother." To have friends like that is to be rich indeed. Not enough? In Ecclesiastes 4:9-12, we read these words: "Two are better than one, because they have a good return for their work: If one falls down, his friend can help him up. But pity the man who falls and has no one to help him up!

Also, if two lie down together, they will keep warm. But how can one keep warm alone? Though one may be overpowered, two can defend themselves. A cord of three strands is not quickly broken."

There are definite benefits for the man who takes the time to build friendships with others. A primary benefit is the growth and maturity that happens in us when we are committed to such a relationship: "Wounds from a friend can be trusted, but an enemy multiplies kisses. . . . Perfume and incense bring joy to the heart, and the pleasantness of one's friend springs from his earnest counsel" (Prov. 27:6, 9). Two delightful expressions here remind us that when genuine friendships are developed, a friend's counsel is helpful and brings joy, but a real friend sometimes tells us what we do not want to hear. In such circumstances, "faithful are the wounds of a friend."

We can grow as men by developing relationships in which we demonstrate loving concern for each other. As we develop this loving concern, we counsel each other. If a relationship has been established, we hear what we need to hear, not just what we want to hear. And because of the relationship, we accept what our friend says and respond accordingly.

One day, Mr. Langton, a good friend of the brilliant Dr. Samuel Johnson, wanted to point out something to Dr. Johnson: "You have a habit of contradicting people in conversation," Langton said.

Johnson responded, "And what's wrong with that?"

"Nothing particularly," Langton said, "except the way in which you do it is hard for sensitive souls to bear."

"If they're sensitive," Johnson responded, "they need to bear something in order to grow up."

The discussion developed into an argument, and Langton decided not to pursue it further. Rather, he chose to write a number of texts on a piece of paper for Johnson. The texts he wrote out were these: "Blessed are the meek." "With all lowliness and meekness . . . endeavoring to keep the unity of the Spirit." "Love suffereth long . . . is kind . . . is not puffed up."

Taking the slip of paper from his friend, who had dared challenge him, Johnson went home. There he read the texts and realized his friend was right. So he returned to Langton and apologized, saying that changes needed to be made. That is friendship—when someone will honestly level with you, giving you the opportunity to know what is wrong and how you can put it right. Friendship takes risks. But counterfeit friendship won't risk at all; people in such relationships simply pretend that everything is fine.

Someone has said, cynically, that there is no man so friendless that he cannot find someone sincere enough to tell him the disagreeable truth. That is true. Unfortunately, some people feel it their God-given responsibility to communicate disagreeable truth to people whom they don't know and therefore cannot possibly care about. My former colleague Joe Ballard once said to me, "Always earn the right to rebuke somebody before you do it." And then he said, "Before you earn the right to rebuke people, you have got to show them that you are primarily concerned with their well-being." Do you have friends like that? If you do not, you are probably remaining at the same level, making the same mistakes, doing the same injurious things, never discovering that a major benefit of friendship is the assurance that someone will be with you in adversity—almost guaranteeing you growth and maturity.

The Privilege of Sharing

Consider these words: "The poor are shunned even by their neighbors, but the rich have many friends. He who despises his neighbor sins, but blessed is he who is kind to the needy" (Prov. 14:20-21). Rich people do have many friends, although the word *friends* might sometimes be questionable. So why is it that celebrities and wealthy people who have lots of people hanging around them sometimes are the loneliest people in the world? Because they constantly wonder if their "friends" are real friends. And often such people feel that it is not them that people want, but their money or the reflected glory of their fame.

Proverbs is absolutely right. The rich have many friends, but the important thing is that those who are kind to the needy are the real friends. A friend in need is a friend indeed. We demonstrate the genuineness of our friendship not by identifying with those who might benefit us, but by identifying with those who need our encouragement and support.

The Price of Friendship

Everything worth something costs something, friendship included.

For example, we must accept the fact that not everyone can be our best friend. You do not have the time and energy to have lots of best friends. And those whom you have decided are going to be your best friends may have no intention of being that. As we have said, friendships operate at different levels.

Let me illustrate this from Jesus' life. When he fed five

thousand men and their families, I am sure that those people were all disposed in a friendly way toward him. If you had asked him then, "Do you have any friends?" he could have said, "Oh, look at my friends—thousands of them all over the place."

He obviously could not develop very close relationships with all of those people, and so out of that great crowd he chose seventy. He spent some time with the seventy, then, having taught them and trained them, he sent them out two by two. Still, seventy is a lot of people to get close to. So he selected twelve and really spent a lot of time with them. When he was in distress and under pressure, he drew to himself three of the twelve. These were his close, intimate friends.

This illustrates how friendships operate at different levels. Friendships grow, mature, and develop. They may start with five thousand, but they will narrow down. Only time and work will determine when and to how many.

Also, when we are making friends, we ought to be aware of the potential dangers. Proverbs is full of healthy warnings in this regard. "My son, if you have put up security for your neighbor [or your friend], if you have struck hands in pledge for another, if you have been trapped by what you said, ensnared by the words of your mouth, then do this, my son, to free yourself, since you have fallen into your neighbor's hands: Go and humble yourself; press your plea with your neighbor! Allow no sleep to your eyes, no slumber to your eyelids. Free yourself, like a gazelle from the hand of the hunter, like a bird from the snare of the fowler" (Prov. 6:1-5). In other words, the best way to lose a friend is to get into a shaky financial deal with him. People change when money comes on the scene! (Someone has said that the best way to lose a friend is to lend him money or sell him your used car.)

Proverbs goes on: "Do not make friends with a hot-tempered man, do not associate with one easily angered, or you may learn his ways and get yourself ensnared" (Prov. 22:24-25). This passage cautions us to be very careful about the friendships we make because they could have a severe impact upon us.

Friendship makes certain demands upon you—reciprocity, honesty, and loyalty. Acceptance is key. If I approach friendship with the idea that I am going to correct somebody, friendship is not going to grow out of the situation. There has to be a basic, mutual acceptance of what we are if friendship is to follow. Friendships are demanding, time consuming, and, frankly, hard work at times. But if we want friends, especially male friends, we must be willing to work at friendship.

Once you have made a friendship, it is important to maintain it. There are four words that need to be emphasized in terms of maintaining friendships.

Caution

"A righteous man is cautious in friendship, but the way of the wicked leads them astray," says Proverbs 12:26. Let us look at some ways in which caution in friendship is imperative.

When I was a teenager, I developed a close friendship with a young married couple who lived a few doors away. I hate to admit that the reason for this deep friendship was that they had gotten one of those newfangled things called a television. I remember my mother sitting me down and quoting Proverbs 25:17: "Seldom set foot in your neighbor's house—too much of you, and he will hate you." That was good advice that I did not want, but I eventually learned to accept it.

Beware of overkill. It is possible to become so smothering and demanding that you destroy the very thing you want to preserve. "If a man loudly blesses his neighbor early in the morning, it will be taken as a curse" (Prov. 27:14). Timing is everything. If you want to maintain a friendship, you do not call your friend at four in the morning to tell him what a neat guy he is.

"Like one who takes away a garment on a cold day, or like vinegar poured on soda, is one who sings songs to a heavy heart" (Prov. 25:20). To be honest, I do not completely understand this verse, but I think it is saying that it is possible for us to be insensitive in our friendships. Often we do not take time to find out how people are feeling. Instead, we transfer our feelings onto them. Here is this poor guy who has a heavy heart and his "friend" comes in all excited, slaps him on the back, punches him in the ribs, and says, "Hey, Buddy, it is great to be alive, isn't it?" "Buddy" replies, "No."

"Like a madman shooting firebrands or deadly arrows is a man who deceives his neighbor and says, 'I was only joking!'" (Prov. 26:18-19). Some people in their friendships begin to demonstrate a certain degree of insincerity. They needle and razz people, getting under their skin, until in the end their former friends tell them to leave them alone.

"We were only kidding," they say. "Can't you take a joke?"

No, they can't take a joke, because there is an element of meanness in this joking from these so-called friends. It is destructive and unkind. The jokers themselves have been insincere. We must guard against overkill, insensitivity, and insincerity if we are to maintain strong friendships.

Commitment

Third John is an interesting letter. It is the shortest book in the Bible, and over and over again in its fourteen verses is the term *dear friends.* If you read this letter, you will get a lovely picture of John, the aged apostle, writing to a group of believers, pointing out now and again that they are all his friends.

Here, John is making a commitment to that fellowship of believers in general, and to individuals in the fellowship in particular. So should we. We should make a commitment to the fellowship of other believers and, on the basis of that commitment, we should give of ourselves in order to build up "dear friend" relationships.

We need these relationships. And they do not happen automatically when we just come into church, sit in our favorite spot, and then go back home. Real friendships happen when there is commitment to the group as a whole, and when we get ourselves into situations where we can nurture more personal, more intimate relationships.

Constancy

"Wealth brings many friends, but a poor man's friend deserts him," states Proverbs 19:4. There is a kind of friendship that will last only until the weather changes.

Constancy becomes especially difficult when we have passed the "comfort" stage of friendship and begin to experience personally the trials and struggles of our friends. Listening is hard and painful work when a friend is going through a death in the family, divorce, financial setbacks, or illness. Yet true friends stay by our side when no one else is willing. And God gives grace, not only to the person going through the trial, but to the person befriending that person.

Candor

Finally, honesty, openness, "speaking the truth in love" is needed. "He who rebukes a man will in the end gain more favor than he who has a flattering tongue" (Prov. 28:23).

Genuine friendship requires honesty. But beware of the wrong kind of candor. "He who covers over an offense promotes love, but whoever repeats the matter separates close friends" (Prov. 17:9). And Proverbs 16:28 says, "A perverse man stirs up dissension, and a gossip separates close friends."

To maintain a relationship, we need to know when to speak and when to keep silent; what to say and what not to say; to whom to speak and to whom not to speak. One of the quickest ways to destroy a friendship is through gossip. This is something we need to guard against. Unfortunately, in the church what passes as candor and speaking the truth in love often is sheer naked gossip, and it is destructive in the extreme.

In closing, some questions: As a man, do you have friends, especially other male friends? Have you devoted the time and effort needed to nurture a few intimate, healthy friendships? If not, are you willing to take the risk? In the friendships you do have, are you cautious, committed, constant, and candid? These are qualities we need to develop.

You are the salt of the earth. But if the salt loses its saltiness, how can it be made salty again? It is no longer good for anything, except to be thrown out and trampled by men.

Matthew 5:13

11

Men Worth Their Salt

"You are the salt of the earth." In a way, these seven words of Jesus encapsulate all that it means to be a real man. Of course they apply to all Christians—men and women. But at this critical time in Western society, I believe they have special significance for men. The fast pace, the economic pressures, and the cultural expectations of today's world can lead us to work so hard at being a good husband, a good father, a good provider, a good friend, that we lose sight of the bigger picture: We are called as Christians to transform the world.

How do we do that? By being salt. Jesus uses this image to illustrate the impact and impression Christians should be making on the society in which they live. As men of God, we are responsible to behave in a distinctively Christian way wherever God has placed us. Our concern should not be with *whether* we are salt—Jesus has already said we are—but whether we are *functioning* as salt.

The Significance of Being Salt

Jesus' listeners, the people of Galilee, knew immediately what he was talking about. For them, salt was not just something in a shiny silver shaker on the dinner table.

Salt preserves. To the people of that day salt was primarily a preservative vital to their way of life. Once they caught a fish, for example, they had to get it to market. And the only way to get it there in marketable condition was to salt it and pack it between layers of salt so they could carry it with them to Jerusalem, where it could be sold as fresh as when they caught it. Salt arrested corruption; it kept fish fresh and edible.

Similarly, we Christians today are to arrest the corruption in our society. Unfortunately, many Christians do not even know what is going on in the world around them; they are unaware of the terrible conditions that exist unchecked. This is one of the reasons we are not making more of a difference in the world around us.

Paul, by contrast, was fully aware of his world when he wrote, "For the message of the cross is foolishness to those who are perishing, but to us who are being saved it is the power of God" (1 Cor. 1:18). "Perishing" aptly describes the condition of society today. The Greek word for "perishing" is the same word used for "lost." People around us are lost, victims of a disease known as sin, which causes their lostness and corruption. Jesus called his followers to be the salt that would halt that condition. If the corruption is not arrested, those who are now in the process of perishing will one day perish for all eternity. Christians are placed in the midst of this perishing, corrupt society to do what we can to stem the tide of godlessness all around us.

There are many ways for us to do this. Some feel it can be done through local government. Others think national politics can make the difference. Still others feel that by being involved in "helping agencies" of one kind or another, they can turn the tide. But the most basic way to do it is to get at the root of corruption in people and help change their condition. Instead of being in the process of perishing, they must be saved. (The problem is inherently spiritual, even though it has social implications and ramifications.) Are we functioning as salt in that capacity?

Salt confirms the promise. Salt has another meaning in the Scriptures. Even today in the Middle East, business agreements and other arrangements are sealed with salt. Numbers 18:19 provides the background of this usage: "Whatever is set aside from the holy offerings the Israelites present to the Lord I give to you and your sons and daughters as your regular share. It is an everlasting covenant of salt before the Lord for both you and your offspring."

As we share with others our experience with Christ, we are passing along this "covenant of salt," this promise of truth. People can "bite into" our experience to test its reality, allowing us the tremendous privilege of being salt to our society. We show to the world, which desperately needs our message, that God is prepared to make a new covenant through the blood of his Son. In 2 Corinthians 3:6 Paul tells us that God "has made us competent as ministers of a new covenant—not of the letter but of the Spirit; for the letter kills, but the Spirit gives life."

Are you and I as Christians truly functioning as salt? Are many people around us coming to grips with the fact that it is possible for God and human beings to be reconciled through Christ's blood, shed on the cross? Do they know it is possible for lostness, corruption, and alienation to be eradicated? That is what it means to be salt.

Salt has positive and negative power. In the Old Testament we learn that it was a military practice in destroying the enemy to sow that city with salt: "All that day Abimelech pressed his attack against the city until he had captured it and killed its people. Then he destroyed the city and scattered salt over it" (Judg. 9:45). This was done so that nothing would ever grow in the area again. This is the way a Christian should function. Our life, our testimony, our very presence should be a positive witness for Christ, but it also should be a negative condemnation to the person who refuses to believe.

Writing to the Corinthians, Paul makes this point: "For we are to God the aroma of Christ among those who are being saved and those who are perishing. To the one we are the smell of death; to the other, the fragrance of life" (2 Cor. 2:15-16). I believe many Christians fall by the wayside because they want to live comfortably. They do not want to upset or perturb anyone. But some people need to be upset and perturbed. What do we do when we see a blind man walking toward a cliff? Do we keep quiet because we do not want to disturb or frighten him? If we do, we are guilty of criminal negligence! If we honestly believe in the corrupting influence of sin and the condemnation of God upon it, then we are responsible to warn the world around us of its danger. Our very quality of life should be a beacon of hope.

According to John, Jesus said, "If you forgive anyone his sins, they are forgiven; if you do not forgive them, they are not forgiven" (20:23). I know there are many interpretations of this, but I believe Jesus was saying, "If you go out into society and tell people, 'Friend, if you refuse to repent, to bow your head and heart before a holy God, if you refuse to acknowledge Jesus Christ as your Savior and Lord, on the authority of the Word of God, you are lost and bound for a Christless eternity,' I will support you from

144

heaven itself." This is what Jesus' words here in John mean to me. Jesus was asking his disciples to function as salt—to affirm his message of condemnation for those who remain in sin, while declaring salvation for the repentant.

Salt purifies. If you have ever had an open cut, you know how salt in that wound made it sting. But it also made it clean. That is another aspect of salt—to purify. For Christians today, that means we are to live lives that are pure, bring about changes in our society that help cleanse it of unrighteousness and impurity, and point constantly to the One who is holy and sinless and blameless, and who invites all sinners to come to him and find forgiveness.

Salt enhances flavor. Job asked the question, "Is tasteless food eaten without salt, or is there flavor in the white of an egg?" (6:6). Did you ever try to eat something that had not been salted to your taste? Flat and unexciting, wasn't it? That is the way many of us Christians come across to people around us—dull. It is what Jesus was referring to when he said, "Salt is good, but if it loses its saltiness, how can it be made salty again? It is fit neither for the soil nor for the manure pile; it is thrown out" (Luke 14:34-35).

Christians have no business being boring. Our function is to add flavor and excitement. If I as a Christian am boring and dull, if I am not adding flavor to life around me, I am not fulfilling my duty as salt.

When I was in the Marines, I was the only one in my group who did not booze it up. Night after night the others would invite me to go out drinking with them, and I would regularly say no to their invitation. Do you know what happened? I became nursemaid and helper, putting them to bed and helping them cope with their hangovers. Yet my example added a little touch of difference to the situation.

It caught their attention, stirred their interest. As the months went by, one by one many of those Marines came to know Christ.

Salt is necessary. The world around us needs Christians to be salt. Our role is not simply to sit back and wait for the bus to pick us up for heaven. God knows how critically important we are to our world here and now. If we are to fulfill our God-given role as salt, we can never settle down to a mundane existence. The flavor of God is desperately needed in our society.

In the Marines, we used to go on speed marches. They were called speed marches because you ran all the way; when you came to a hill, you ran twice as fast! The only thing we had to eat on those marches was salt, actual chunks of it. Perspiration would blind us, but as long as we had the salt, we could go on. Without it we could not survive. In the Middle East, salt is one of the most precious commodities available. The body requires salt in order to function. In Jesus' day, as now, the mineral was vital and pivotal to the lifestyle of the people.

What an exciting concept! You and I as Christians are vital to the world around us. We can say, "O God, if those in my little piece of the world are to survive, they actually need me to be salt." That gives Christianity a totally new dimension.

Salt is distinctive. Christians are to stand out from the crowd. They are to be different in their approach to life. When the world around us seems bent on its own destruction or indifferent to its own danger, we Christians are to stand up and be counted—not just for the sake of being different, but to be the "salt" that preserves and purifies. We live by principles put in place by God, and the world around us desperately needs to know this.

Salt is abrasive. In Judges 18:7, a certain little town is described this way: "So the five men left and came to Laish, where they saw that the people were living in safety, like the Sidonians, unsuspecting and secure. And since their land lacked nothing, they were prosperous. Also, they lived a long way from the Sidonians and had no relationship with anyone else."

Everyone in Laish was living comfortably, lacking nothing and possessing wealth. In the face of an approaching enemy, they remained unconcerned. As a result, they who were living comfortably perished comfortably! If only there had been one man who had stood to his feet and shouted, "Fools! Wake up!" Of course the people would have been upset at one who rocked the boat like this. They might have called him an oddball. But he might have saved their lives.

This is the kind of abrasive character we Christians are to have. We are to confront people around us—in love— with the truth that stands in total contrast to the lies that are lulling them to sleep. That is what it means to be a Christian. And that is what it means for Christians to be salt.

The Seriousness of Being Salt

This brings us to the "but" of our opening verse: "You are the salt of the earth. But if the salt loses its saltiness . . ." Here Jesus is getting around to the importance of fulfilling our function as salt. There is disgrace and possible disaster here in terms of our Christian testimony. The possibility that the salt may lose its savor was hinted at by Paul in Romans: "Although they claimed to be wise, they became fools" (1:22). Although there is apparently nothing about salt in this passage, in the original Greek it is the same language Jesus used when pointing out that salt could go flat.

In Galilee, where Jesus lived at this time, a cheap grade of salt was used for packing fish. Once it lost its saltiness, it was useless. If it was spread on the ground, nothing would grow. If it was thrown in the water, it just made the water dirty. This "nonsalt" was not good for anything. Jesus was warning his listeners that if they were not careful, they too could lose their edge, their distinctiveness, and their power. I have heard the term "good for nothing" applied to a variety of people. But Jesus applies it to saltless Christians! It is possible for a Christian to be good for nothing but to be trampled underfoot.

As Christian men, are we functioning as salt or are we just fooling around? We can fool around by being more concerned about "spiritual correctness" than about changing the world for Christ. We can fool around by being more interested in social conformity than in spiritual impact. We can also fool around by being more intent on making a good impression than on having real influence for the kingdom.

Every value and every role we have examined in this book plays a vital part in the making of a true man of God, a real man of honor and influence. But let us never forget that all those parts fit into a larger divine purpose. God in Christ is reconciling the world to himself, and we are his instruments of reconciliation—beginning with our own hearts, and extending out to our families, friends, neighbors, coworkers, and all of society.